The New Three-Year
Garden Journal
with regional gardening guides

LOUISE CARTER & JOANNE SEALE LAWSON

PHOTOGRAPHS BY ALLEN ROKACH

FULCRUM PUBLISHING ⚛ GOLDEN, COLORADO

FOREWORD

Gardening efforts yield the best results when carried out in a timely manner. To the novice gardener, the number of tasks to be accomplished may be overwhelming without a step-by-step guide, and the experienced gardener may tend to procrastinate if not reminded of what needs to be done. *The New Three-Year Garden Journal* offers a wealth of gardening information and design ideas to guide both the novice and the experienced gardener in planning and recording the gardening year.

The week-by-week gardening guide, organized into seven geographical regions, reflects the great diversity of climate and plant material in the United States and neighboring regions of Canada. This catalog of ideas and reminders can be adapted to the needs of every gardener.

I invite you to read and enjoy this journal, to record in it, and be guided by it to a more beautiful garden and a more bountiful harvest.

CARL TOTEMEIER
The New York Botanical Garden

Book design by Angela Overy.

Printed in Italy

0 9 8 7 6 5 4 3 2 1

Fulcrum Publishing
350 Indiana Street, Suite 350
Golden, Colorado 80401-5093 USA
(800) 992-2908 • (303) 277-1623
e-mail: fulcrum@fulcrum-gardening.com
website: www.fulcrum-gardening.com

Library of Congress Cataloging-in-Publication Data

Carter, Louise.
    The new three-year garden journal : with regional gardening guides / Louise Carter, Joanne Seale Lawson : photographs by Allen Rokach.
        p.   cm.
    Rev. ed. of: The three year garden journal. 1989.
    ISBN 1-55591-392-X (hardcover)
    1. Gardening—United States. 2. Gardening—United States—Calendars. I. Lawson, Joanne Seale. II. Rokach, Allen. III. Carter, Louise. Three year garden journal. IV. Title.
SB453.C336   1998
635.9'0973—dc21   98-20536
                                         CIP

CONTENTS

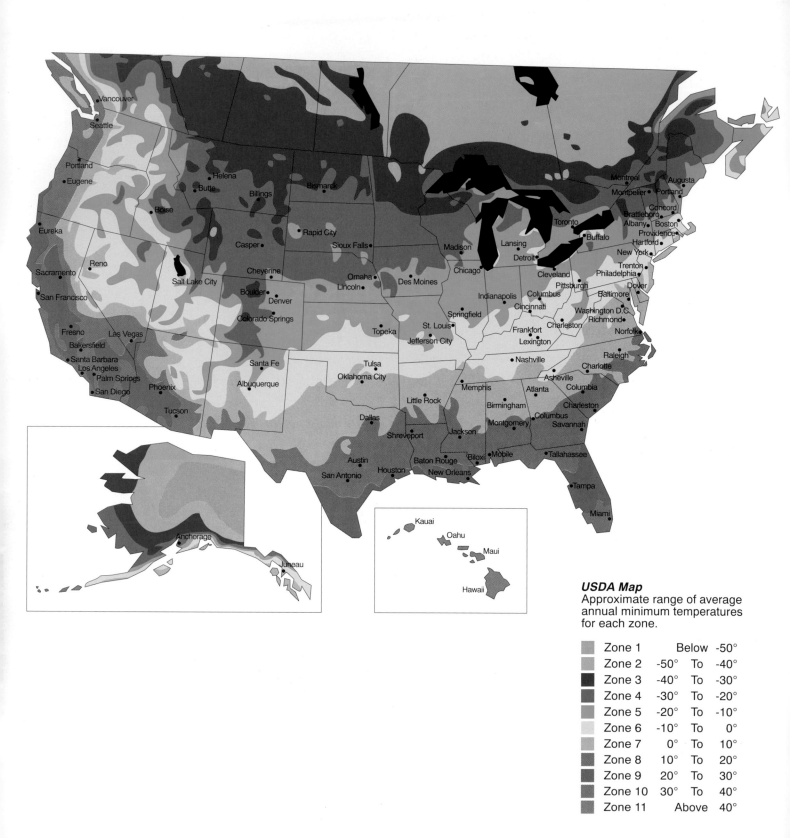

USDA Map
Approximate range of average annual minimum temperatures for each zone.

	Zone 1		Below	-50°
	Zone 2	-50°	To	-40°
	Zone 3	-40°	To	-30°
	Zone 4	-30°	To	-20°
	Zone 5	-20°	To	-10°
	Zone 6	-10°	To	0°
	Zone 7	0°	To	10°
	Zone 8	10°	To	20°
	Zone 9	20°	To	30°
	Zone 10	30°	To	40°
	Zone 11		Above	40°

This is a national journal that provides specific, monthly, zone-by-zone gardening information keyed to the U.S. Department of Agriculture Plant Hardiness Zone Map for the continental United States and neighboring sections of Canada. Most plant material mentioned in this journal will grow throughout the continent, though some will take different forms in different regions. For example, an annual in New England may be a perennial in Florida, and a reliably hardy vine in California will need winter protection in Colorado. In case of doubt, consult your local agricultural agent or a nearby garden center.

- As the gardening year progresses, use this journal to record your ideas and observations. Note what is blooming, berrying, or changing color. Note, too, any clashing combinations or dull times.

- Educate your eye.

- Study gardening books and magazines.

- Visit well-planted gardens to study design solutions and styles.

- Take photographs to record plant and color combinations you find pleasing.

- Stop at local garden centers weekly to see what is in bloom and being offered for sale.

- Consider consulting landscape design or horticultural experts for additional suggestions or enrolling in a course in ornamental horticulture at a local college.

- In the fall, evaluate this year's gardening efforts, review your records, and continue to put your ideas into action.

- Use the garden highlights section found in the regional notes each month as an additional guide to enrich your garden and give it year-round interest. With careful planning, there will always be highlights in your garden.

We urge you to refer to the Appendix for more complete instructions on carrying out the various year-round gardening tasks—planting, pruning, fertilizing, and general maintenance—recommended each month for the seven regions covered in this journal.

Northeast
USDA zones 4, 5, 6, and all or part of the states of Connecticut, Illinois, Indiana, Iowa, Kentucky, Maine, Massachusetts, Michigan, Minnesota, Missouri, New Hampshire, New Jersey, New York, Ohio, Pennsylvania, Rhode Island, Vermont, West Virginia, Wisconsin, and neighboring sections of Canada.

Mid-Atlantic
USDA zone 7 and all or part of the states of Arkansas, Delaware, District of Columbia, Georgia, Kentucky, Maryland, Massachusetts, Mississippi, New Jersey, North Carolina, Oklahoma, Pennsylvania, Rhode Island, South Carolina, Tennessee, Texas, and Virginia.

Mid-South
USDA zone 8 and all or part of the states of Alabama, Georgia, Louisiana, Mississippi, North Carolina, South Carolina, and Virginia.

Gulf & South Atlantic Coasts
USDA zones 9 and 10 and all or part of the states of Alabama, Florida, Georgia, Louisiana, Mississippi, South Carolina, and Texas.

Pacific Southwest & the Desert
USDA zones 7, 8, 9, 10, and all or part of the states of Arizona, California, Colorado, Nevada, New Mexico, Oklahoma, Texas, and Utah.

Pacific Northwest
USDA zones 7, 8, 9, and all or part of the states of California, Oregon, Washington, and neighboring sections of Canada.

Rocky Mountains & the Plains
USDA zones 4, 5, 6, and all or part of the states of Arizona, Colorado, Idaho, Kansas, Montana, Nebraska, Nevada, New Mexico, North Dakota, Oregon, South Dakota, Texas, Utah, Washington, Wyoming, and neighboring sections of Canada.

A Design for All Seasons

Gardens are as variable as the gardeners who design and tend them. A garden should be a source of year-round beauty and pleasure. If you find that your garden does not meet these criteria or is in some sense unsatisfying, January presents the perfect opportunity to analyze its bare-bones design qualities without the distraction of leaves, flowers, and berries.

Walk around your home, sit in the yard, stand on the terrace or patio, look out the windows—upstairs and down. Assess your property's strengths—a grove of handsome trees, a well-placed garden pool, a sheltered sunny nook, a pleasant view. Assess its weaknesses—an exposed site, a heavily shaded dank pocket, overgrown or boring plants, an unpleasant view. Your design solution should reflect the results of this analysis.

The soil, the climate, and the site of your garden are predetermined. Although each of these conditions can be modified to a degree, they should suggest ways to approach the design of your garden as well as influence your choice of plants.

Keep in mind, too, how you and your family use the property and the amount of space, time, and energy you have for gardening. Gardens and gardeners change over time as they mature. An open play yard can become a woodland path with shade-loving plants as playground equipment gives way and trees fill out. A large grassy area can become a formal flower garden or a more casual meadow. A good basic landscape plan can accommodate changes in need and taste.

Ask yourself, "Does my garden have a theme that unites the various elements?" Interest in a specific type of plant material, such as roses, perennials, herbs, alpines, or dwarf evergreens, might lead to a design that highlights them. Or, a garden could be developed around a color scheme: a white, silver, and gray flower garden, or a chartreuse and purple shrub border. Because of your work schedule, your choice might be a garden to be enjoyed at a particular time—evenings, weekends, or one season of the year—a spring wildflower garden, for example. Knowledge of a historical period or gardening style—Persian, Italian, French, English, Japanese, American colonial—might inspire the integration of their signature components, the use of water, architectural elements, and plant material in a fresh and original form. Beware if these elements are not understood or if they are impractical to maintain.

But remember, above all, that your garden needs a dominant theme and style to produce a successful and unified landscape that is in keeping with your climate, your property, and your neighborhood.

Northeast
Snow and ice prevail

Mid-Atlantic
Snow and ice prevail

Mid-South
Frost is possible

Gulf & South Atlantic Coasts
Late frost is possible

Pacific Southwest & the Desert
Late frost is possible

Pacific Northwest
Frost is possible

Rocky Mountains & the Plains
Freezing temperatures continue

year _____ _____

GARDENING GUIDE ~ PLANTING

Northeast

INDOORS: Plant paperwhite narcissus in pebbles and water. Sow lettuce, arugula, corn salad, basil, Italian parsley to grow under fluorescent light. Bring well-rooted, spring-flowering bulbs indoors from cold frame or basement to force bloom. Fertilize house plants showing signs of growth. Check for insects, diseases.

Mid-Atlantic

INDOORS: Plant paperwhite narcissus in pebbles and water. Sow lettuce (bibb, black-seeded Simpson, buttercrunch, oakleaf) to grow under fluorescent light. Fertilize house plants showing signs of growth. Check for insects, diseases.

Mid-South

OUTDOORS: Begin to plant, transplant deciduous and broadleaf and needle evergreen trees, shrubs, vines, bare-root roses, fruit and nut trees, asparagus from two- to three-year-old roots while dormant if weather permits and ground is friable. Sow cool-season vegetables, annuals in cold frame. INDOORS: Check house plants for insects, diseases; repot ferns.

Gulf & South Atlantic Coasts

OUTDOORS: Begin to plant, transplant trees, shrubs, vines, roses, ground covers, summer-blooming bulbs as they become available in nurseries. Set out seedlings or sow cool-season annuals, vegetables, herbs. *Zone 9:* sow warm-season vegetables, herbs in cold frame (or flats indoors) to transplant out after last frost. Plant precooled tulips.

Pacific Southwest & the Desert

OUTDOORS: Plant, transplant trees, shrubs, vines, roses, ground covers while dormant, bare-root fruit and nut trees, berries, perennial vegetables, strawberry plants. Set out cool-season annuals. In cold frame (or flats indoors)—*zone 9:* sow warm-season vegetables, herbs; *zone 8:* sow cool-season vegetables, herbs.

Pacific Northwest

OUTDOORS: Plant, transplant trees, shrubs, vines, roses, perennials, ground covers while dormant, if weather permits. Plant bare-root fruit and nut trees, berry bushes, strawberries, artichokes, asparagus, horseradish, rhubarb. Sow cool-season vegetables in cold frame (or flats indoors).

Rocky Mountains & the Plains

INDOORS: Plant paperwhite narcissus in pebbles and water. Check spring-blooming bulbs; if well rooted, bring indoors to bloom. Sow lettuce, arugula, corn salad, basil, Italian parsley to grow under fluorescent light. Fertilize house plants showing signs of growth. Check for insects, diseases. Pull plants back at night to protect from icy, drafty windows.

PRUNING

Northeast

Prune deciduous plants while dormant, including berry bushes, grapevines. Prune early spring-flowering shrubs and trees for branches to force into bloom indoors. Call an arborist for major tree work.

Mid-Atlantic

Prune deciduous plants while dormant, including berry bushes, grapevines. Prune early spring-flowering shrubs and trees for branches to force into bloom indoors. Call an arborist for major tree work.

Mid-South

Prune deciduous plants and evergreen woody plants while dormant, including fruit trees, berries, figs, grapes, kiwis. Do not prune spring-flowering plants or flower buds will be lost. Prune tree limbs damaged by ice and snow. Cut ornamental grasses to 6" before new growth begins.

Gulf & South Atlantic Coasts

Prune deciduous plants and evergreen trees, shrubs, and hedges, early fruit trees, kiwis, grapevines, berries while dormant, if not done in fall. Save bloom buds by limiting pruning of spring-flowering trees and shrubs to removal of suckers and winter-damaged growth. Begin annual heavy pruning of shrub roses as buds swell. Cut back or mow ornamental grasses, liriope, mondo grass before new growth begins.

Pacific Southwest & the Desert

Prune deciduous and evergreen trees, fruit trees, summer- and fall-blooming shrubs, hedges, vines while dormant. Cut back winter-damaged plants, including root-hardy tropicals, fuchsias. To save bloom buds, limit pruning of spring-flowering trees and shrubs to removal of suckers and winter-damaged growth. Begin annual heavy pruning of shrub roses as buds swell. Cut back ornamental grasses, perennials. Mow unkempt ground covers.

Pacific Northwest

Prune deciduous and evergreen trees and shrubs, shrub roses, fruit trees, grapevines, berries, currants, perennials, ornamental grasses before new growth begins. Do not prune spring-blooming shrubs until after bloom. Mow unkempt ground covers. Prune early spring-flowering shrubs for branches to force into bloom indoors.

Rocky Mountains & the Plains

Prune deciduous plants while dormant, including summer- and fall-blooming trees and shrubs, fruit trees, berry bushes, grape-vines. Prune early spring-flowering shrubs for branches to force into bloom indoors. Call an arborist to schedule major tree work.

year _____

FERTILIZING & GARDEN HIGHLIGHTS

Northeast

Feed dormant acid-loving plants if not fed in late fall. Spray newly planted evergreens with antidesiccant when temperature is above 40°.

> *Highlights.* Winter interest: lingering berries, colorful and exfoliating bark, plant silhouettes.

Mid-Atlantic

Feed dormant acid-loving trees and shrubs if not fed in late fall. Spray broadleaf and newly planted needle evergreens with antidesiccant.

> *Highlights.* Winter interest: broadleaf and needle evergreens, colorful and exfoliating bark, plant silhouettes, buds, pods.

Mid-South

Apply dormant oil spray. Spray newly planted evergreens with antidesiccant. Watch for signs of overwintering insects, borers, scale.

> *Highlights.* Bulbs: aconite, crocus, snowdrop; perennials: hellebore, violet; shrubs: sasanqua and Japanese camellias, winter honeysuckle, winter jasmine, wintersweet.

Gulf & South Atlantic Coasts

Fertilize cool-season annuals, emerging perennials, strawberries, citrus, tropical fruit trees, winter vegetables. Apply dormant oil spray.

> *Highlights.* Early bulbs: daffodil, iris; cool-season annuals, perennials, and flowering trees and shrubs.

Pacific Southwest & the Desert

Fertilize established plantings, annuals, emerging perennials. Apply dormant oil spray, pre-emergent herbicides, fungal sprays.

> *Highlights.* Early bulbs; perennials: hellebore; cool-season annuals; shrubs: camellia, jasmine; trees: acacia, purple orchid tree.

Pacific Northwest

Fertilize cool-season annuals, emerging perennials, fruits. Apply dormant oil spray. Spray for peach leaf curl.

> *Highlights.* Early bulbs; perennials; shrubs: camellia, daphne, heather, rhododendron, viburnum, winter jasmine, witch hazel.

Rocky Mountains & the Plains

Feed dormant acid-loving plants if not fed in late fall. Spray evergreens with antidesiccant when temperature is above 40° to protect from moisture loss.

> *Highlights.* Winter interest: needle evergreens, plant silhouettes, colorful and exfoliating bark, buds, pods.

GARDEN MAINTENANCE

Northeast

Check winter plant protection from sunscald, frost heave, rodent damage. Shake or sweep snow from evergreens. Let icy covering melt naturally. Water newly planted and established broadleaf and needle evergreens during January thaw. Plan spring improvements. Feed resident birds mixed seed and suet. Check stored bulbs and tubers.

Mid-Atlantic

Check winter plant protection: tree wrap, wire mesh set against rodent damage, guy wires. Use discarded Christmas tree boughs to protect tender plants from winter burn and frost heave. Use sand or ashes on icy walks and drives—salt damages plants. To prevent indelible footprints, avoid walking on frozen grass. Feed resident birds mixed seed and suet. Check stored bulbs and tubers.

Mid-South

Check winter plant protection. Remulch beds to protect tender plants from sunscald, frost heave. Prepare vegetable garden if ground is frost-free. Inventory garden supplies. Study plant and seed catalogs and order for spring and summer plantings. Feed resident birds mixed seed and suet. Lawn care—*lower South:* apply lime, top-dress low areas.

Gulf & South Atlantic Coasts

Begin spring cleanup. Begin removing winter plant protection. Begin watering as plants break dormancy. Prepare planting beds. Mulch figs. Service irrigation systems. Study plant and seed catalogs and order for spring and summer plantings. Lawn care: apply pre-emergent herbicide to warm-season grasses, treat for brown patch if necessary.

Pacific Southwest & the Desert

Mulch and protect tender plants in beds and containers. Begin spring cleanup. Prepare planting beds. Water in dry areas. Check stored bulbs and tubers. Service irrigation systems. Study seed catalogs and order for spring and summer plantings. Lawn care: fertilize cool- and warm-season grasses, annual rye.

Pacific Northwest

Prepare planting beds if ground is frost-free and not soggy. Mulch tender plants, figs. Service irrigation systems. Plan spring improvements. Study seed catalogs and order for spring and summer plantings. Check stored bulbs and tubers.

Rocky Mountains & the Plains

Water broadleaf evergreens, roses monthly during a thaw if snow cover is light. Check winter plant protection. Use discarded Christmas tree boughs to protect tender broadleaf evergreens from sunscald and small plants from frost heave. Avoid walking on frozen grass. Study plant and seed catalogs for spring and summer plantings. Feed resident birds mixed seed and suet. Check stored bulbs and tubers.

DESIGNING WITH PENCIL AND PAPER

Sound design principles and a good basic structure underlie all successful spaces, both indoors and out. A well-designed garden of any size is a series of connected outdoor spaces. Just like your house, it is equipped with the outdoor versions of floors, walls, and ceilings. Each area, or "room," should have a specific purpose, fulfill a specified need, stand on its own, and yet be a harmonious part of a larger composition.

Ask yourself some questions. Are these rooms well located, defined, and of a usable size? Is there a sitting area with easy access to the living room or kitchen? Can it accommodate a comfortable arrangement of furniture for the family and guests? Do these outdoor spaces flow easily together? For instance, can the children reach their play equipment without running through the sitting area? Are the sunny areas planned for flowers, herbs, and vegetables and the shady ones for entertaining and relaxing? How about screening? Is there a swimming pool, is it an eyesore for many months of the year, or is it tucked away behind a hedge? Are there out-of-sight but convenient places for a compost pile, for a cold frame, for storing gardening supplies, firewood, and trash? Is there a place for water in the garden? Water, even in a small bird bath, fountain, pool, or stream, adds life to a garden and, when moving, creates sounds that mask distracting outside noises.

Is the garden furnished with comfortable all-weather furniture for lounging or dining? Are there decorative containers, statues, and fountains to act as focal points? Is there adequate lighting at night to provide a pleasant atmosphere outside and to create a vista—instead of a black hole—when the garden is viewed from inside the house?

Are there strong edges and boundary walls that give the property a sense of enclosure and privacy? Boundaries can be composed of hedges, fences, walls, or handy outbuildings, such as a garden or tool shed. Privacy is especially important in a small garden. Don't neglect overhead elements, such as the canopy of a tree beside a patio, or arbors and trellises, which not only provide a home for flowering vines but also create a sense of intimacy and scale while offering protection from the sun, wind, and rain.

Do the paved areas (hardscape), including terraces, walks, steps, and driveways, and the planted areas (greenscape), including lawn and planting beds, form pleasant shapes that tie together and complement each other? Think of the lawn as a positive design element, not just that space left over after the planting areas have been laid out. All paved and green areas should be well graded, drained, and comfortable to walk or drive on, not quagmires of mud or ice when it rains or snows. Within a garden, steps and retaining walls can create interest as well as control erosion and poor drainage, transforming slopes into usable level ground.

Take note of environmental conditions, of areas that are exposed or sheltered, sunny or shady, always wet or dry, where existing plants do not thrive, and other places that are difficult to maintain. You will be able to resolve these problems by modifying these conditions and choosing the right type of plant for the site.

Is the entrance to your house inviting? Can the house be glimpsed from the street? Is the front walk easy to locate and is it wide enough for two people to walk side by side? Are the front steps of equal height and in good repair? Is there a railing? If there is a side entrance, is it clearly marked? Is the parking for family and visitors adequate and out of sight of the living areas? At night are the house number, front walk, and driveway well lighted? Is the planting in scale, or has it outgrown its surroundings, threatening to engulf the path or cover the first-floor windows?

Is the property handsome in all seasons? Is there a pleasing mix of evergreen and deciduous plant material? Does everything bloom at once or is it staggered for bloom and color throughout the year? Are plants arranged in pleasing groups emphasizing the major lines of the design, or are they scattered about like remnants at a nursery? It is tempting to have one of everything, but resist this urge unless you have an arboretum. Restraint is the key to harmony.

Most important, do all the separate elements—hedges, planting beds, retaining walls and steps, arbors, lawns, and service areas—relate to the house and to each other?

This garden leads the eye along the foliage beds and path to an attractive vista.

After you have analyzed your garden, draw a landscape plan. It will be an invaluable document for planning future improvements. A camera can be a useful tool. Take photographs of any view that doesn't please you or an area that doesn't work. Stand in one spot, perhaps with your back to the house looking toward the rear yard, or stand across the street from your front entrance. Take a series of photographs from left to right of the view before you. Tape them together to create a panoramic sweep. Place tracing paper over these collages and experiment by sketching different design solutions on the paper. Try different arrangements of trees and shrubs, "build" a wall, add a planting bed.

Once you have chosen a solution, move out into the actual landscape. Place tall stakes where you think you would like trees, shorter ones to represent shrubs. Use the garden hose to outline a planting bed or the curve of a walk. Set the garden furniture out on the grass where you are planning the new terrace. Mock up a fence or retaining wall using stakes of the appropriate height and colored twine to represent the top elevation. Drive your car into the area designated for a driveway or parking area to see if you can enter and exit easily. Sit on the "terrace," sit under the new "tree," try out the "walk." Check your solutions for size and shape and your views from all angles, including the upstairs windows. Make as many adjustments as necessary until you are satisfied. By this trial-and-error method, you will avoid costly and time-consuming mistakes.

Obtain a scaled survey, or plat, of your property, which will locate your house in relation to property lines and the street or sidewalk. Enlarge it to a workable scale, such as 1/4 inch = 1 foot (which means 1/4 inch on the plan equals 1 foot on the ground) or a 1/8-inch scale for a large property. Lay a piece of transparent graph paper over the enlarged plan and draw in the trees, shrubs, planting beds, terrace, walks, driveway, and service areas you worked out on the ground.

Now consider different planting schemes. In a region with marked seasonal changes, think in terms of the four seasons. In a milder climate, emphasize winter screening and spring, summer, and fall color to prevent monotony.

The combination of foliage color and textures, plant shapes, and brick path make this an interesting design.

If you have a small garden, you may want to concentrate on one or two spectacular flowering times. Choose enough plants from each season to make a show. Winter is often ignored by gardeners, but it is crucial to a successful design. In winter a garden must have a firm and balanced framework. Make sure the evergreens and deciduous plants are well distributed over the property. Think of plants in a group, not as individuals, and use them in sweeps and masses. Spring is next; until the weather settles, make sure early bloom is visible from indoors. In summer, flowers should be visible from the terrace, pool, or other outdoor living areas. In summer, you will also need well-placed trees to provide shade for living areas. Fall is the final season; imagine views to be enjoyed from the windows as you move back inside.

Color the plant selections in your plan, using a different color for each season. Try dark green for evergreens, pink for spring-bloomers, yellow for summer, and orange for plants that provide a fall show. Visit your local arboretum, public garden, or garden center to see what is in bloom during the different seasons.

Once you have drawn a landscape plan, you can add to it as the whole panoply of the gardening year unfolds before you.

Naturalized daffodils emerging in spring just as the trees are starting to leaf out.

Bulbs for All Seasons

From the first snowdrop in late winter to the last autumn-blooming crocus, flowering bulbs bring color, gaiety, and ephemeral beauty to the garden. As the snow melts, the small bulbs—snowdrop, winter aconite, snow crocus, chionodoxa, and anemone blanda—appear naturalized in colonies under shrubs, between tree roots, or in the lawn. In wild gardens, iris reticulata, species tulips, and trout lilies bloom before the trees leaf out and are followed by lilies of the valley and Spanish bluebells.

Bulbs get larger and blooms more extravagant as days lengthen and the season advances. At the edge of the lawn, sweeps of daffodils follow the early bulbs in company with grape hyacinth and fritillaria. In borders the sculptural quality of hybrid tulips and Oriental hyacinths lends a formal note. Bearded iris, handsome in bloom, leave their swordlike, silvery foliage as an accent in the garden, and Japanese iris thrive near the water.

Summer arrives with agapanthus, alliums, tuberous begonias, and early lilies. Crocosmia and blackberry lily add texture and color to perennial borders. Then come the hot colors of exotic gladiolus and cannas and the cooling respite of variegated caladium leaves bobbing gently in the shadows. In spacious borders, hybrid lilies add a grand and voluptuous note, while the long, curving spikes of eremurus wave dramatically against dark green hedges.

With the approach of fall, dahlias and lycoris provide a last burst of color before bulbs diminish in size and blooms return to the softer, paler colors of colchicum, autumn crocus, and sternbergia, which blend with the richness of fall foliage and late-blooming perennials. Hardy cyclamens are the last to appear before winter arrives.

Indoors, nothing is more cheerful in winter than a bowl of paperwhite narcissus planted in pebbles and water, or more fragrant than a single hyacinth in bloom in a glass vase on a sunny windowsill. Amaryllis adds a festive holiday note and clivia provides handsome foliage before its rich orange blossoms present a splash of color in late winter. Coming full circle, in southern gardens and northern greenhouses, freesia and calla lilies are in bud.

Northeast
Snow and ice prevail

Mid-Atlantic
Freezing temperatures continue

Mid-South
Frost is possible

Gulf & South Atlantic Coasts
Danger of frost continues

Pacific Southwest & the Desert
Danger of frost continues

Pacific Northwest
Danger of frost continues

Rocky Mountains & the Plains
Snow and ice prevail

GARDENING GUIDE ~ PLANTING

Northeast

INDOORS: Sow slow-growing annuals, vegetables indoors in flats. Take geranium cuttings to plant out in May, June. Check house plants frequently for insects and diseases, groom, fertilize if showing signs of growth, turn in window for even development.

Mid-Atlantic

INDOORS: Sow slow-growing annuals, vegetables in flats or jiffy pots to set out after last frost. Take cuttings of geraniums to plant out in May, June. Check house plants regularly: groom, turn in window for even development, watch for insects and diseases and treat promptly.

Mid-South

INDOORS: Sow warm-season annual and tender perennial seeds in flats to plant out after last frost. Start caladiums in pots. OUTDOORS: Sow warm-season vegetables, herbs in cold frame. Continue to plant bare-root, b & b, container-grown trees, shrubs, roses, vines while dormant. Sow cool-season annuals or set out seedlings.

Gulf & South Atlantic Coasts

OUTDOORS: Complete dormant planting. Plant and dig to rejuvenate summer-, mid-fall-blooming perennials. Sow and set out cool-season annuals. *Zone 10:* continue to plant summer-blooming bulbs; sow all vegetables and herbs. *Zone 9:* sow and set out cool-season vegetables and herbs; plant perennials, vegetables, strawberries; start warm-season annuals, vegetables in cold frame (or flats indoors).

Pacific Southwest & the Desert

INDOORS: Sow warm-season annuals, biennials, vegetables in flats. In cooler areas start summer-blooming bulbs in pots to set out when danger of frost is past. OUTDOORS: Continue dormant planting; divide perennials; in warmer areas set out cool-season annuals, vegetables, summer-blooming bulbs.

Pacific Northwest

INDOORS: Sow cool-season annuals in flats. Start summer-blooming bulbs in pots to set out in May. Check house plants for insects and diseases, groom well, cut back, divide, and repot overgrown plants. Fertilize plants showing signs of growth. OUTDOORS: Continue permanent plantings. Sow cool-season vegetables, herbs.

Rocky Mountains & the Plains

INDOORS: Sow cool-season annuals, vegetables, herbs in flats. Take geranium cuttings to plant out in May, June. Check house plants frequently for insects and diseases, groom well, cut back, divide, and repot overgrown plants. Fertilize plants showing signs of growth.

year _____

PRUNING

Northeast

Continue dormant pruning of trees, summer- and fall-blooming shrubs, berry bushes, grapevines. Renewal-prune overgrown shrubs. Limb up multistemmed shrubs to expose handsome bark and stems. Save bloom buds by limiting pruning of spring-blooming trees and shrubs to removal of suckers and growth damaged by ice and snow.

Mid-Atlantic

Continue dormant pruning—include ornamentals, fruit trees, berry bushes, grapevines. Save bloom buds by limiting pruning of spring-blooming trees and shrubs to removal of suckers and growth damaged by ice and snow. Finish pruning maples, birch, dogwoods, which bleed if pruned later, or wait until summer.

Mid-South

Continue winter pruning. Limit pruning of spring-flowering trees and shrubs to removal of suckers and winter-damaged growth. Prune shrub roses as buds swell. Shape hedges. Cut back ornamental grasses, liriope, ground covers before new growth begins. Limb up multistemmed shrubs to expose handsome bark and stems (crape myrtle, nandina, yaupon). Prune for softwood cuttings as new growth appears.

Gulf & South Atlantic Coasts

Continue winter pruning and removal of storm-damaged limbs when new growth reveals extent of damage. Complete annual heavy pruning of shrub roses. Shape hedges. Deadhead bulbs as they finish blooming, but leave foliage to yellow and wither to nourish bulbs. Prune for hard- and softwood cuttings.

Pacific Southwest & the Desert

Complete winter pruning. Renewal-prune overgrown shrubs. Limb up multistemmed shrubs and small trees to reveal handsome bark and stems. Finish pruning winter-damaged trees, shrubs, root-hardy tropicals, fuchsias. Complete annual heavy pruning of shrub roses.

Pacific Northwest

Complete dormant pruning of woody plants, including berry bushes, grapevines, fruit trees. Complete annual heavy pruning of shrub roses. Limb up multistemmed shrubs and small trees to reveal interesting bark and stems. To save bloom buds, limit pruning of spring-flowering trees and shrubs to removal of suckers and growth damaged by ice and snow.

Rocky Mountains & the Plains

Continue dormant pruning of woody plants, including berry bushes, grapevines, fruit trees. Save bloom buds by limiting pruning of spring-blooming shrubs and trees to removal of suckers, growth damaged by ice and snow. Renewal-prune overgrown shrubs. Shape hedges.

FERTILIZING & GARDEN HIGHLIGHTS

Northeast
Reapply antidesiccants to broadleaf and newly planted needle evergreens if temperature is above 40°.

Highlights. Bulbs: aconite, snow crocus, snowdrop; perennials: hellebore; shrubs: Chinese witch hazel, heath, winter honeysuckle, winter jasmine, wintersweet.

Mid-Atlantic
Apply dormant oil spray to fruit trees, ornamentals when temperature is above freezing.

Highlights. Early bulbs: aconite, snow crocus, snowdrop; perennials: hellebore, skunk cabbage; shrubs: cornelian cherry, daphne, heath, pussy willow, winter honeysuckle, winter jasmine, wintersweet, witch hazel.

Mid-South
Fertilize established trees, shrubs, emerging perennials and bulbs.

Highlights. Early bulbs; perennials: hellebore, pansy, primrose, rockcress; shrubs: almond, daphne, forsythia, mahonia, pieris, pussy willow, quince, spirea; trees: cornelian cherry, shadbush, star magnolia, witch hazel.

Gulf & South Atlantic Coasts
Fertilize trees (including citrus), shrubs, vines, ground covers, perennials, winter annuals.

Highlights. Early bulbs: cymbidium; cool-season annuals; perennials: Iceland poppy, phlox, snapdragon, sweet pea, violet; shrubs: honeysuckle, jasmine; trees: acacia, cherry, crabapple, redbud, star and saucer magnolias.

Pacific Southwest & the Desert
Fertilize established trees, shrubs, vines, ground covers, perennials. Apply iron chelates if necessary.

Highlights. Early bulbs: cymbidium; cool-season annuals; climbers: Carolina jasmine, thunbergia; shrubs: azalea, camellia, mahonia, osmanthus, pieris, quince, early spirea, winter daphne; fruit trees.

Pacific Northwest
Fertilize established trees, shrubs, vines, ground covers, perennials, berry bushes, figs.

Highlights. Early bulbs: aconite, crocus, daffodil, snowflake; perennials: hellebore; shrubs: daphne, mahonia, PJM rhododendron, shadbush, viburnum, winter hazel, witch hazel.

Rocky Mountains & the Plains
Watch for signs of overwintering insects and diseases, including borers, caterpillar nests, galls, scale.

Highlights. Early bulbs: aconite, snow crocus, snowdrop; perennials: hellebore; shrubs: Chinese witch hazel, heath, winter honeysuckle, winter jasmine, wintersweet.

year _____ _____

GARDEN MAINTENANCE

Northeast

Loosen winter mulches matted by snow. Check winter plant protection, stakes, and ties. Reapply antidesiccants. Open and ventilate cold frames if temperature is above 45°. Clean, sharpen, oil tools. Inventory supplies. Order flower and vegetable seeds, perennials, bare-root plants for April planting. Feed birds.

Mid-Atlantic

Check winter plant protection. Install a cold frame to protect tender plants. Inventory supplies. Service lawn mowers, spray equipment. Order disease-resistant flower and vegetable seeds, perennials, bare-root trees and shrubs for April planting. Scrub pots and flats to be used for seedlings.

Mid-South

Begin spring cleanup: start a compost pile, gradually remove winter screens and mulches. Remove excess Spanish moss with rake or by hand and compost. Open and ventilate cold frames when temperature is above 45°. Lawn care: fertilize cool-season grasses, apply pre-emergent crabgrass control.

Gulf & South Atlantic Coasts

Begin spring cleanup: remove winter mulches, start a compost pile for clean refuse, rake up and dispose of fallen azalea leaves, camellia blooms. Begin rose care program. Finish plant orders for spring planting. Plan fall bulb order to fill vacant spots as they appear. Lawn care: top-dress low spots, apply pre-emergent herbicides.

Pacific Southwest & the Desert

Remove winter mulches gradually and compost. Prepare beds for spring planting if ground is friable. Continue to water regularly. Lawn care: fertilize cool- and warm-season grasses, apply pre-emergent crabgrass control.

Pacific Northwest

Install a cold frame to protect tender plants and for starting seedlings. Begin spring cleanup: start a compost pile, gradually remove winter screens and mulches. Rake up and prepare beds for spring planting. Lawn care: fertilize cool- and warm-season grasses, apply pre-emergent crabgrass control.

Rocky Mountains & the Plains

Check winter plant protection. Reapply antidesiccant to young evergreens if temperature is above freezing. Water broadleaf and needle evergreens during a thaw if snowcover has been light. Combat insects in dry areas by washing evergreens well with a strong blast of water. Continue to feed birds.

Designing with Bulbs

Most bulbs are easy to grow and should be included as seasonal additions to your basic garden plan. If different species are chosen, bulbs will provide blooms throughout most of the year. Pleasing color combinations can be worked out on graph paper. Make notes in the spring about where you intend to plant bulbs in the fall to bloom the following year.

Learning about their native habitats will enable you to use bulbs with confidence. Most hardy spring bulbs (snowdrop, crocus, some scilla, trillium, and most daffodils and lilies) are native to regions with wet winters, freezing temperatures, and frequent snowcover. They can withstand being frozen and require, or tolerate, rain in the summer. They thrive and naturalize if left in the ground in northern climates. In southern climates these bulbs must be planted anew each year. Many other well-known bulbs (gladiolus, freesia, sparaxis, tritonia, ixia, babiana, amaryllis, clivia, and agapanthus) are native to South Africa with its mild winters and long dry summers. These are tender bulbs that must be heavily mulched, lifted, and stored, or grown indoors in colder climates.

For simplicity, true bulbs, as well as corms, tubers, and rhizomes, are referred to as "bulbs" in the following discussion because their methods of treatment and roles in the garden are similar. All bulbs store food and moisture in an underground organ, an adaptation that allows them to survive inhospitable conditions of drought and cold in their native habitats. All bulbs restore themselves through their foliage, which must be left to wither naturally before being removed. All bulbs require good drainage; planting on hillsides, mounds, or in raised beds helps meet this requirement. Camassia is an exception and will grow in damp meadows. Most bulbs prefer sunshine. Once planted they should be left in the garden, unless they are too tender to survive winter cold or summer heat and are therefore used as bedding plants. If bulbs are to be removed, lift them once their growing cycle is completed and store them until the next planting season. If bulbs are crowded, transplant them in the garden just after they bloom, when they are easily found, so that they can establish themselves before going dormant.

Because most gardens contain microclimates—small areas that are cooler or warmer than the norm—sites can be found for a variety of bulbs, or conditions can be adapted to suit their needs and encourage growth. Beware of automatic watering systems, which may cause them to rot.

In cold climates, early spring-blooming bulbs need protected settings. In rock gardens or against a warming stone wall, plant masses of winter aconite (*Eranthus* spp.), snowdrops (*Galanthus* spp.), dwarf daffodils, or crested iris (*Iris cristata*) for bright spots of color as the snow melts. Set them close to the house under early-flowering shrubs where they can be seen from the window until the weather settles, or beside the kitchen or front door where they can be enjoyed as you come and go. Delicate species crocus naturalized in the lawn will bloom and fade before the grass needs mowing. Squill (*Scilla*) and chionodoxa will spread and, planted in companionship with vinca minor, will produce sheets of blue and violet among the shallow roots of maple and beech trees. These small bulbs go well with hellebore, violets, epimedium, brunnera, and the earliest wildflowers.

Daffodils look their best planted in large drifts at the edge of the lawn, in front of a grove of trees, along a stream, or in a meadow. Planted in large numbers, they can be enjoyed from afar and their foliage left to ripen where its untidiness will not be objectionable. Daffodils mix well with grape hyacinth (*Muscari* spp.) or squill for contrast, and with the less formal species or wild tulips. In southern gardens, plant precooled daffodil bulbs. The lack of sufficiently low temperatures during winter months denies daffodils the cold period they require for proper plant formation. Bulbs left in the garden will not rebloom.

In more limited spaces, in small gardens, and in large containers, plant bulbs in layers for a long sequence of bloom. Begin with fritillarias at the bottom, then tulips in the next layer, hyacinths next, and Dutch crocus on top. Each set of foliage will be larger than the previous one and will conceal what came before.

Following the early wild tulips, which are appropriate in the rock or wild garden, hybrid tulips, their more glamorous descendants, show off well in formalized plantings. Under a flowering tree, in front of the shrub border, or in formal beds, set Dutch tulips in blocks of a single color in waving ribbons, tone against tone: white against red against purple. Or choose bulbs of the same color but different species to contrast shapes: pink hyacinths with pink tulips.

In early summer in wild gardens or mixed borders, native trillium, trout lilies, and jack-in-the-pulpit will thrive in light shade. Martagon and leopard lilies and wood hyacinths (*Scilla campanulata*) will add bright patches of color to more open glades in the woods.

Snowflakes (*Leucojum* spp.) and ornamental onions (*Allium* spp.) bridge the gap between spring- and summer-blooming bulbs, the former bobbing on tallish stems like long-legged snowdrops and the latter producing unexpected flower shapes such as drumsticks *(A. altissimum)*, clusters of small round balls *(A. mollis)*, or large heads of star-shaped flowers on top of 4- to 5-foot stems *(A. giganteum)*. Flower colors vary from white to yellow to mauve depending upon the variety.

Overplant spring bulb beds with summer-blooming annuals or perennials—impatiens, hosta, and ferns—to disguise yellowing bulb foliage. Ornamental grasses are a perfect companion to bulbs as they will rise early to enhance plantings of mixed spring bulbs and continue to develop from summer into fall, finally producing decorative seed heads that persist into winter. In semishady spots along the edge of the meadow or on sunny banks where daffodils bloomed earlier, plant daylilies, which withstand drought and heat. Choose varieties with different blooming times for several months of color.

Throughout the summer, in containers on decks, terraces, and roof gardens or in hanging baskets and window boxes, summer-blooming bulbs offer contrasting shapes and vivid color. Lilies will bloom over several months if different varieties are planted. They are a glorious addition to the perennial bed or shrub border and can be grown in containers. In the Deep South, lily bulbs must be lifted in the fall and refrigerated for six to eight weeks or they might not bloom again next year. Plant lily-of-the-Nile (*Agapanthus africanus*) in tubs by the swimming pool; tuberous begonias in hanging baskets to decorate the porch; lilies, dahlias, gladiolus, and cannas to stand tall at the back of the perennial border; blackberry lilies (*Belamcanda chinensis*) and watsonia to add delicacy and grace to a mixed planting. Caladiums, with their variegated leaves, are useful with ferns and hostas in shady corners in the garden and in containers. In colder areas these tender bulbs, with the exception of blackberry lilies, must be rescued for winter storage. In warmer climates they can be left in the ground to naturalize. Amaryllis and clivia, which naturalize in southern gardens, are popular indoor flowering bulbs in the North.

In late summer, fall-blooming colchicum and lycoris, which bloom after their foliage has disappeared, work well as flowering companions to plumbago, asters, and Japanese anemones. Save a spare colchicum bulb to flower indoors, lying bare on a glass-topped table.

For indoor color in winter, pot up precooled hardy bulbs for forcing. Daffodils, tulips, hyacinths, and crocus are traditional, but snowdrops, Dutch and reticulated iris, grape hyacinth, aconite, *Scilla tubergeniana,* and lily of the valley can all be forced to bloom before their normal season in the same manner. Brodiaeas and ornithogalums, though not classified as hardy bulbs, can also be forced; they can be potted in a large container for a miniature garden. Planted at two-week intervals, these bulbs can be grown close together in a flat and used for cuttings indoors. If leftover bulbs are a hardy variety, they can be planted outdoors in the vegetable garden in rows for cutting in the spring.

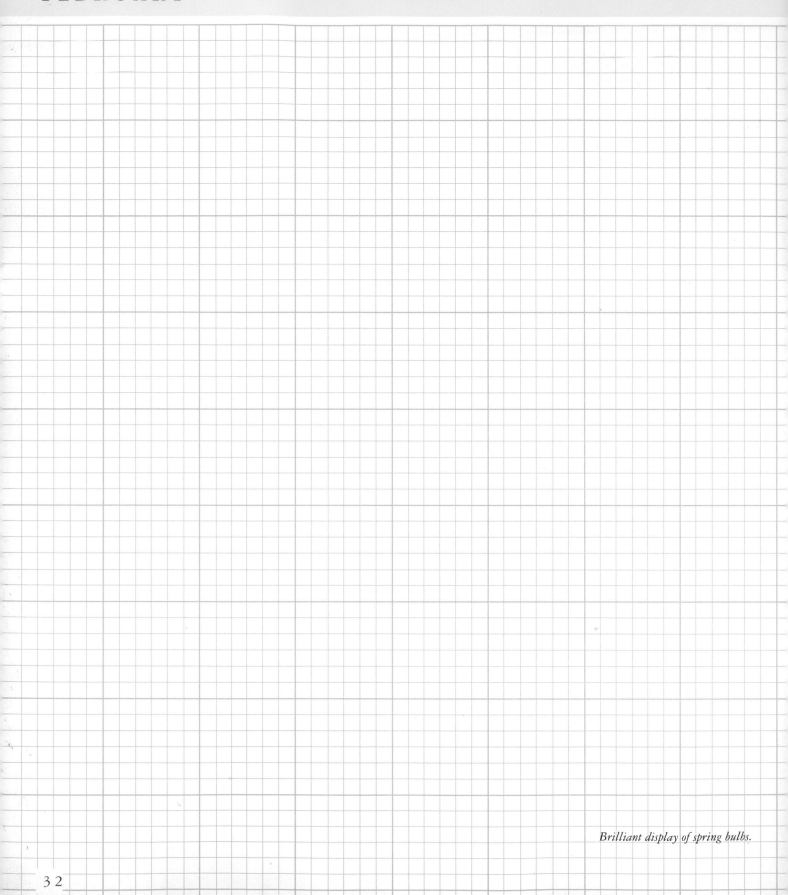

Brilliant display of spring bulbs.

Carefully selected shrubs enhance a spring woodland scene.

TREES FOR ALL SEASONS

Trees are the most prominent and permanent vertical element in any landscape. They constitute the upper or canopy layer of the garden. Trees give a sense of place—the pungent, shaggy eucalyptus of California, the stately firs of the Northwest, moss-covered oaks of the South, snowclad aspen of the Rocky Mountains, loblolly pines along a Texas highway, palms swaying in a tropical breeze, sugar maples in a New England fall, dogwood and redbud in bloom in the Virginia Piedmont. You have only to look and smell the air to know where you are.

There are deciduous trees and needle and broadleaf evergreen trees. Trees come in a vast array of sizes, shapes, and foliage patterns and colors. Deciduous trees can be multistemmed like birch, or single-trunked like ash and hickory. There are vase-shaped elms and zelkovas, weeping willows and cherries, horizontally branched hawthorns and dogwood, or columnar cypress and poplar. Most evergreen trees like holly, spruce, and cypress are pyramidal in form.

Tree foliage varies in density from the heavy-headedness of lindens to the delicate leafy branches of the moraine locust. The arching fronds of palms are decorative and fanciful while the foliage of beech is gracefully layered. The leaf texture of many Japanese maples are finely cut, that of goldenrain coarse and compound. Among broadleaf evergreens, magnolia foliage is a shiny, leathery, dark green, that of holly, spiny and curved. The foliage of needle evergreens, pine, fir, and spruce, is finely textured, that of cypress and arbovitae fan-shaped.

Many small deciduous trees, crabapples, Japanese magnolias, cherries, pears, dogwoods, and acacias, have distinctive spring or summer blossoms and appealing fall fruit and foliage colors. After leaf fall the colorful and interesting bark of birch, parrotia, Oriental dogwood (*Cornus kousa*), stewartia, and many maples is revealed. Maples, oaks, sycamores, and willows as well as pines and spruce add movement and sound to the garden when the wind blows through their leaves.

In winter, deciduous trees cast the shadows of their bare branches on a wall or stand silhouetted against the sky. Needle evergreens in northern climates take on richer colors, greens, grays, blues, and golds deepen against the dark sky. They come into focus when there is little else of interest in the garden. In warmer climates broadleaf evergreens, live oak, arbutus, holly, and magnolia continue to provide leaves of differing shapes and color from gray through variegated to a rich glossy green.

Northeast
Freezing temperatures continue

Mid-Atlantic
Freezing temperatures continue

Mid-South
Frost is possible

Gulf & South Atlantic Coasts
Late frost is possible

Pacific Southwest & the Desert
Late frost is possible

Pacific Northwest
Frost is possible

Rocky Mountains & the Plains
Freezing temperatures continue

GARDENING GUIDE ~ PLANTING

Northeast

INDOORS: Sow cool-season vegetables, annuals in flats. Continue house-plant care. *Zone 6:* sow warm-season vegetables, summer-blooming annuals in flats. OUTDOORS: Plant, transplant deciduous and evergreen trees and shrubs while dormant. Plant bare-root plants. Sow cool-season annuals, vegetables.

Mid-Atlantic

INDOORS: Sow cabbage family, warm-season vegetables in flats. Continue house-plant care. OUTDOORS: Transplant deciduous and evergreen plants while dormant. Dig and divide summer- and winter-blooming perennials. Sow cool-season annuals, vegetables. Plant asparagus, rhubarb, berry bushes, grapevines.

Mid-South

INDOORS: Sow annuals, perennials in flats. Continue house-plant care. OUTDOORS: Plant, transplant permanent plantings. Divide and rejuvenate summer- and fall-blooming perennials. Begin planting summer-blooming bulbs. Sow cool-season vegetables. Set out warm-season vegetable seedlings with protection.

Gulf & South Atlantic Coasts

INDOORS—*Zone 9:* start summer-blooming bulbs, caladiums, dahlias to set out after danger of frost. Repot orchids. OUTDOORS: Continue permanent plantings. Plant tropical and subtropical plants, annuals. Plant cool- and warm-season vegetables and herbs. Continue to plant summer-, fall-blooming perennials. Begin to divide winter-blooming perennials.

Pacific Southwest & the Desert

INDOORS: Sow tender annuals, start tender bulbs in flats. OUTDOORS: Plant summer-blooming bulbs, lilies after danger of frost is past. Continue to plant perennials, divide existing ones. Plant or sow annuals, vegetables. *Zones 10, 9:* plant citrus, palms, tropicals, subtropicals. *Zone 7:* begin permanent plantings.

Pacific Northwest

INDOORS: Continue house-plant care. Sow tender annuals. *Zone 8:* continue to start summer-blooming bulbs. OUTDOORS: Complete dormant planting. Continue planting broadleaf and needle evergreens, vines, ground covers. Transplant or sow cool-season crops. Sow warm-season crops in flats to set out in May.

Rocky Mountains & the Plains

INDOORS: Sow cool-season vegetables, annuals in flats. *Zone 6:* sow warm-season vegetables, summer-blooming annuals. Continue house-plant care. OUTDOORS: Transplant deciduous and evergreen trees and shrubs while dormant. Plant bare-root berry bushes, grapevines, asparagus, hardy vegetable seedlings. Sow hardy annuals, vegetables.

year _____

PRUNING

Northeast

Prune winter-damaged hedges to green wood. Trim broader at top than bottom to allow more light to reach lower branches. Complete annual heavy pruning of shrub roses as buds swell. Clip established ivy. Cut ornamental grasses to 6" before new growth begins.

Mid-Atlantic

Prune winter-damaged hedges to green wood. Trim broader at top than bottom to allow more light to reach lower branches. Complete annual heavy pruning of shrub roses as buds swell. Clip established ivy. Cut ornamental grasses to 6" before new growth begins.

Mid-South

Prune winter-damaged trees and shrubs. Continue pruning shrub roses. Deadhead cool-season annuals, early spring-flowering bulbs, but leave bulb foliage to yellow and wither to nourish bulbs.

Gulf & South Atlantic Coasts

Prune and lightly shear spring-flowering shrubs, vines, shrub roses as they finish blooming. Prune fuchsias before new growth appears. Continue to deadhead bulbs. Trim evergreens that are putting out new growth.

Pacific Southwest & the Desert

Prune spring-flowering shrubs, vines, shrub roses as they finish blooming. Trim evergreens putting out new growth. Deadhead early annuals, spring-blooming bulbs, but leave bulb foliage to yellow and wither to nourish bulbs.

Pacific Northwest

Prune established hedges, spring-flowering shrubs, vines as they finish blooming. Complete annual heavy pruning of shrub roses. Deadhead early spring-blooming bulbs, but leave foliage to yellow and wither and nourish bulbs.

Rocky Mountains & the Plains

Continue pruning of summer-blooming shrubs, winter-damaged hedges. Prune shrub roses as buds swell. Limit pruning of spring-flowering shrubs and trees to removal of suckers, winter-damaged or crossing branches to save blossom buds.

year _____

FERTILIZING & GARDEN HIGHLIGHTS

Northeast

Fertilize trees, shrubs, ground covers if not fed in late fall, rhubarb, asparagus, berries, grapes. Apply dormant oil spray.

> *Highlights.* Bulbs: aconite, chionodoxa, crocus, daffodil, dwarf iris, snowdrop, windflower; wildflowers: marsh marigold, skunk cabbage, spring beauty; shrubs: pussy willow.

Mid-Atlantic

Fertilize trees, shrubs, ground covers, vines, perennials, established bulb beds, rhubarb, asparagus, berries, grapes.

> *Highlights.* Bulbs: chionodoxa, daffodil, dwarf iris, scilla, windflower; shrubs: early azaleas, camellia, mahonia, pieris, quince, rhododendron; trees: birch, shadbush.

Mid-South

Fertilize trees, shrubs, ground covers, perennials, annuals, bulbs as they finish, berries, grapes, figs.

> *Highlights.* Bulbs: tulip, wood hyacinth; early perennials; climbers: Carolina jasmine, Cherokee rose, clematis; shrubs: azalea, camellia, deutzia, viburnum; trees: fruit trees, magnolia.

Gulf & South Atlantic Coasts

Fertilize trees, shrubs, perennials, vines, bulbs, annual and vegetable seedlings, palms, tropical foliage plants.

> *Highlights.* Early summer-blooming bulbs, including epiphytic orchids; early annuals and perennials; many vines, flowering trees and shrubs.

Pacific Southwest & the Desert

Fertilize new annual beds, bulbs as they finish blooming, vegetable seedlings. Complete fertilizing of trees, shrubs, vines, ground covers, perennials.

> *Highlights.* Early bulbs; cool-season annuals; perennials: cymbidium, iris, wildflowers; shrubs: azalea, cassia, forsythia, pieris, raphiolepis; fruit trees.

Pacific Northwest

Complete feeding of established trees, shrubs, vines, ground covers, perennials, bulbs as they finish blooming. Apply iron chelates if necessary.

> *Highlights.* Early bulbs: daffodil, grape hyacinth; early perennials; shrubs: pieris, forsythia, spirea, spring heather, viburnum; trees: fruit trees, star magnolia.

Rocky Mountains & the Plains

Fertilize trees if not fed in fall, shrubs, ground covers. Apply sulphur to combat high pH. Apply pre-emergent crabgrass control. Apply dormant oil spray.

> *Highlights.* Early bulbs: crocus, daffodil, snowdrop; shrubs: forsythia, mahonia; trees: elm, maple, willow.

Garden Maintenance

Northeast

Begin removing winter mulches, plant screen. Prepare beds for spring planting. Continue to feed the birds. Lawn care—*Zone 6:* apply pre-emergent crabgrass control; begin major work—test soil, adjust pH to 6.5, rake, top-dress, seed bare spots, fertilize established lawns, water frequently; start a new lawn from seed or sod.

Mid-Atlantic

Begin spring cleanup: remove winter mulches, early weeds. Prepare annual beds. Ventilate cold frame when temperature is above 45°. Lawn care: apply pre-emergent weed control; begin major work; fertilize established lawns; start a new lawn from seed or sod; begin mowing when grass is 3" high.

Mid-South

Continue removing winter mulches and add to compost. Begin moving annuals, perennials to cold frame to harden off. Begin summer rose care program. Lawn care: begin major work—test soil, adjust pH to 6.5, correct drainage, top-dress, seed bare spots, fertilize established lawns, water frequently.

Gulf & South Atlantic Coasts

Begin rose care program. Move annual and vegetable seedlings to cold frame to harden off before planting out in garden. Move house plants outdoors once danger of frost is past. Lawn care: begin major work—cut grass severely; thatch, rake and remove clippings; test soil; adjust pH to 6.5; correct drainage; plug, sod, or seed new lawns; fertilize established ones.

Pacific Southwest & the Desert

Begin spring cleanup. Weed and edge beds. Begin rose care program: deadhead, fertilize monthly, spray, water regularly. Tie up berry canes for easier harvesting. Set cutworm collars. Lawn care: begin major care of cool-season grasses; fertilize established lawns.

Pacific Northwest

Prepare annual and perennials beds, vegetable garden. Continue moving hardy seedlings to cold frames to harden off before planting out. Mulch newly planted and established plants to 2"—4". Begin rose care program: deadhead, fertilize monthly, spray, water regularly. Lawn care: begin major work; feed or sod new lawns; fertilize established ones.

Rocky Mountains & the Plains

Begin spring cleanup: remove winter mulches. Prepare beds for spring planting. Irrigate after severe winter storms. Begin hardening off seedlings. Lawn care—*zone 6:* begin major work—test soil, adjust pH to 6.5, rake, top-dress, seed bare spots, fertilize established lawns, water frequently; start a new lawn from seed or sod.

DESIGNING WITH TREES

When refining the planting scheme for your garden, begin with the trees. Trees not only provide shelter, privacy, and shade, but your choice of trees will determine the character and sense of scale of your property. Trees are the link between your property and the neighborhood. "Borrow" trees in the adjacent landscape and include them visually in your composition. If you plant trees that are native to or common in your area, you will blur property boundaries and achieve a greater sense of space. In rural areas, this practice will also soften the abrupt change between a cultivated and natural landscape. Save the more exotic specimens for intimate areas closer to the house.

Site trees with care, considering their eventual spread, soil, and moisture requirements. Major trees (40–100 feet high, 20–40 feet wide) relate the house to the sky. They stand above the shrubs and grass, setting the framework for the rest of the garden. Ornamental trees (15–40 feet high and just as broad) relate the house to the ground plane. Plant major trees as least 20 feet from the house, and minor trees as least 10 feet from it. Select trees whose eventual height and width will stay in scale with the house and not require extensive pruning. When possible have trees of both sizes on a property to give a sense of diminishing scale. To preserve a feeling of space, keep trees with colorful foliage in the foreground and those with cooler colors—blues and grays—in the distance.

A pleasing mix of evergreen and deciduous plant material will contribute summer as well as winter interest. Deciduous trees let in the warmth of the winter sun but give summer shade. Evergreens provide a background for the ornamental trees as well as a winter windscreen and year-round privacy.

Choose plants that are reliably hardy in your area suitable for your soil conditions—acid or alkaline, wet or dry. Make sure they are resistant to local insects and diseases, urban pollution, salt air, humid or arid conditions.

Lengthen the blooming season by choosing varieties that bloom at different season. Red maple *(Acer rubrum)*, cornelian cherry *(Cornus mas)* and serviceberry *(Amelanchier* sp.) bloom in late winter, followed by the early magnolias, fruit trees, dogwoods, fringe tree *(Chionanthus virginicus)*, yellowwood *(Cladrastis kentukea)*, catalpa, and linden. Stewartia, goldenrain *(Koelreuteria paniculata)*, and sophora mark summer, sourwood *(Oxydendron arboreum)*, evodia *(Evodia Daniellii)*, and franklinia the onset of fall. Some ornamental trees, dogwoods, crabapples, and hawthorn lengthen the season by providing colorful fall fruits and foliage.

In a large garden, a row of trees will create a formal atmosphere, or divide and compartmentalize spaces while providing a sense of enclosure. Use trees to define the boundaries, determine an axis, or frame a view. They can be sheared and trained into a tall hedge. A pair of fastigiate deciduous trees or columnar needle evergreens can serve to frame a gateway or view. In a small garden, a single tree can dominate and will determine the scale of the entire property. One or two round-headed trees may suffice to block out an unwanted view and screen you from your neighbors. Small trees with a spreading habit, those with multistems, and particularly those with attractive flowering and fruiting and foliage habits at different seasons, make good focal points in any small garden situation. Informal clumps of trees can locate an entrance, soften the edges of the house, provide a focal point or a sense of mystery. In tight situations ornamental trees can be espaliered against a wall. In a vegetable garden, dwarf fruit trees can be grown in containers or trained on wires to act as a fence enclosing the vegetables.

Tie groups of trees together with sweeps of ground cover, tall grasses, or masses of shrubs to give them more emphasis in the overall design. Placing trees in planting beds eases maintenance and protects trunks from being scarred by lawn mowers. Take into account that tree roots often spread beyond the drip line of the tree (the extent of the canopy) and determine what can be planted under them. Shallow-rooted trees—beech, maple, dogwood—will accommodate spring-flowering bulbs and ground covers but not grass. Deeply-rooted trees—oaks, sourgum, and zelkova—allow more leeway for shrubs and perennials. Some trees—fruit trees, ash, catalpa, deciduous magnolias—are messy and not suitable for the patio or pool area.

Trees can be pruned for interest. Hornbeam, linden, crabapple, and laburnum can be pleached—trained by pruning and interweaving their branches—to form an arching canopy or hedge along a walk. Sycamore, linden, catalpa, and willow trees can be pollarded—trained by having all the main limbs cut back to the trunk—to produce a mass of large leaves and small branches, and a compact crown. Trees, especially yew and holly, can be pruned into formal and amusing topiaries or clipped into standards. In a tight situation, espalier trees against a bare wall to add ornamental interest. Fruit trees are traditional candidates, but almost any small tree can be pruned in this fashion. Limb up stewartia, saucer magnolia *(Magnolia soulangiana),* paperbark maple *(Acer griseum),* parrotia, and lacebark pink *(Pinus bungeana)* by removing their lower branches to reveal interesting bark and growth habits. Some needle evergreens, such as black pine and juniper, lend themselves to being clipped and trained into sculptural specimens.

Major shade trees can also be limbed up. To relieve crowding or to reveal a view, remove the lower limbs of tall trees. Continue removing lower limbs as the trees grow taller. Their trunks will become columns, giving a feeling of height and grandeur. Thin out the tops of heavy trees to allow more light to reach the ground and to develop bright, sunny spots on a woodland where flowering shrubs, perennials, ferns, and bulbs can flourish.

If a tree you inherited with the property is ugly, or becomes ugly because of storm damage or disease, if it is planted in the wrong place, or hangs dangerously over the house, or is a fire hazard, do not hesitate to cut it down. A garden has no place for a poor or misplaced plant that annoys you or compromises your design. Replace it with one that you can watch grow with pleasure and that will contribute to the overall beauty of your garden.

Using trees with varied color and texture to create a backdrop and divide up the gardening bed adds interest to the landscape.

This exquisite tree makes a focal point for the whole garden.

SHRUBS FOR ALL SEASONS

Shrubs are the backbone of most gardens, filling the intermediate layer between the canopy of trees and the soil level of ground covers and grass. The demarcation line between large shrubs and small trees is blurred because some trees are naturally multistemmed and some shrubs grow taller than small trees. In general, a shrub is a woody plant with a number of stems rising from the base, as opposed to a tree, which has a single trunk. They can be depended on to carry a garden through the seasons and even through periods of neglect.

Shrubs provide texture, patterns, form, and color. They contour and outline garden species and create a sense of privacy and enclosure. Like patio trees, they relate the house to the garden, and people to the house. They establish scale in all dimensions: depth, width, and height. They can be planted formally as hedges or informally in natural masses. Shrubs produce their blossoms at or below eye level.

Shrubs can be used individually or in small groups to make divisions within the garden, give background to flower beds, define paths and borders, accentuate doorways and entrances; or they can be planted in masses as low ground covers. They moderate the climate within the garden, sheltering people and tender plants from wind and sun. They obscure unsightly views and muffle distracting noises.

Shrubs, like trees, are either evergreen or deciduous. Evergreen shrubs, broadleaf and needle, provide continuity and permanence throughout the year. Deciduous shrubs add the excitement of seasonal change to the landscape. It is this category that includes many of the spectacular spring- and summer-blooming shrubs.

Because they herald spring, winter-blooming shrubs are the most welcome. They are often extremely fragrant. One specimen of wintersweet *(Chimonanthus praecox),* witch hazel *(Hamamelis mollis),* early-blooming viburnum, or daphne is enough to perfume a garden, and a branch brought inside can perfume an entire room. In warm climates, fall-blooming sasanqua camellias blend fall into winter, and spring-blooming Japanese camellias blend winter into spring. In late spring and through the summer, flowering shrubs add continuous color, height, and texture to the flower border. Lilacs, fothergilla, spireas, weigelas, azaleas, and rhododendrons fill spring gardens. Roses, viburnums, hydrangeas, fuchsias, oleander, gardenia, buddleia, hypericum, potentilla, and vitex follow in the summer. Fall brings the bloom of sweet-smelling osmanthus and elaeagnus, followed by displays of fruits and brilliant foliage color.

Northeast
Danger of frost continues

Mid-Atlantic
Danger of frost continues

Mid-South
Danger of frost continues

Gulf & South Atlantic Coasts
Weather extremes possible

Pacific Southwest & the Desert
Hot weather possible

Pacific Northwest
Danger of frost continues

Rocky Mountains & the Plains
Last frost is possible

Gardening Guide ~ Planting

Northeast

INDOORS: Transplant warm-season vegetables to larger containers. Pot up summer-blooming bulbs for planting out in May. *Zones 5, 4:* sow vegetables, annuals. OUTDOORS: Plant, transplant all hardy plant material. Divide crowded early bulbs, summer- and fall-blooming perennials.

Mid-Atlantic

INDOORS: Sow basil, remaining annual seeds. Pot up summer-blooming bulbs. OUTDOORS: Plant, transplant bare-root and container-grown roses, ground covers, daylilies, cool-season annuals and vegetables, strawberries. Divide crowded spring-blooming bulbs, summer- and fall-blooming perennials. Sow cool- and warm-season vegetables and herbs.

Mid-South

OUTDOORS: Continue permanent plantings. Continue to plant summer-blooming bulbs, divide crowded perennials. Plant container plants, hardy and tropical water lilies. Start biennials, perennials in cold frame for fall planting. Sow or transplant vegetables, herbs to garden.

Gulf & South Atlantic Coasts

OUTDOORS: Continue to plant container-grown plants, tropical and semitropical plants, water lilies. Finish planting summer-blooming bulbs. Continue to plant summer-blooming annuals, divide crowded perennials. Plant container plants, window boxes, hanging baskets. Set out or sow warm-season vegetables, herbs.

Pacific Southwest & the Desert

OUTDOORS: Continue permanent plantings, including tropical and semitropical plants. Set out summer-blooming bulbs. Continue to plant annuals, divide crowded summer- and fall-blooming perennials, spring-blooming bulbs. Plant hardy and tropical water lilies. Set out or sow warm-season vegetables, herbs.

Pacific Northwest

OUTDOORS: Continue permanent plantings. Set out summer-blooming bulbs. Begin planting summer-blooming annuals. Divide and rejuvenate perennials, crowded bulbs. Plant hardy water lilies. Sow cool- and warm-season vegetables. Set out warm-season vegetable seedlings once danger of frost is past.

Rocky Mountains & the Plains

INDOORS: *Zone 5*—sow warm-season annuals, vegetables; pot up summer-blooming bulbs for planting out in May. OUTDOORS: Plant, transplant all hardy plant material, including cool-season annuals, hybrid lilies, water lilies, vegetables. Divide summer- and fall-blooming perennials, crowded early bulbs. As ground warms, sow cool-season annuals, vegetables, herbs.

PRUNING

Northeast

Prune trees, shrubs. Continue pruning shrub roses. Shear or mow winter-damaged ground covers to 5". Deadhead bulbs but leave foliage to yellow and wither to nourish bulbs.

Mid-Atlantic

Prune trees, shrubs except spring-bloomers. Shear or mow winter-damaged ground covers to 5". Deadhead early bulbs but leave foliage to yellow and wither to nourish bulbs.

Mid-South

Shear or hand-prune trees, shrubs lightly as they finish blooming. Pinch chrysanthemums monthly. Pinch runners on new strawberry plants. Continue to deadhead bulbs and leave foliage to wither naturally before removing.

Gulf & South Atlantic Coasts

Continue to shear spring-flowering plants lightly as they finish blooming. Do not prune shrub roses. Prune needle evergreens putting out new growth. Deadhead, pinch back annuals to encourage continuous bloom, perennials (especially chrysanthemums, fuchsias) to delay bloom. Continue to deadhead bulbs and leave foliage to wither.

Pacific Southwest & the Desert

Prune needle evergreens putting out new growth. Continue to hand-prune spring-flowering trees, shrubs. Continue to deadhead spring-blooming bulbs.

Pacific Northwest

Prune evergreens putting out new growth. Continue to shear spring-flowering plants lightly as they finish blooming. Continue to deadhead bulbs.

Rocky Mountains & the Plains

Continue to prune shrub roses as buds swell. Limit pruning of spring-blooming shrubs, trees to removal of dead or diseased wood to save bloom buds. Shear or mow winter-damaged ground covers to 5". Deadhead bulbs but leave foliage to yellow and wither naturally to nourish bulb.

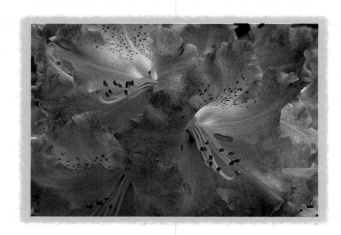

FERTILIZING & GARDEN HIGHLIGHTS

Northeast

Fertilize emerging perennials lightly.

Highlights. Bulbs: aconite, chionodoxa, crocus, daffodil, dwarf iris, snowdrop, windflower. *Zone 6*—wildflowers: marsh marigold, skunk cabbage, spring beauty; shrubs: pussy willow.

Mid-Atlantic

Fertilize ground covers, emerging perennials lightly, bulbs as they finish blooming.

Highlights. Bulbs: allium, anemone, Dutch crocus, fritillaria, hyacinth, species tulip; early perennials; early shrubs; trees: cherry, crabapple, plum, star magnolia.

Mid-South

Fertilize annual and vegetable seedlings, bulbs as they finish blooming. Spray fruit trees.

Highlights. Bulbs: allium, crinum, lily, lily of the valley, ranuncula, scilla, tulip; annuals; perennials; climbers: clematis, honeysuckle, wisteria; flowering shrubs and trees.

Gulf & South Atlantic Coasts

Fertilize azaleas, camellias, bulbs as they finish blooming, annuals, summer-blooming bulbs, container plants. Feed fruit trees, vegetables for second time.

Highlights. Late bulbs, annuals, perennials, climbers, and shrubs; trees: acacia, cassia, citrus, coral tree, evergreen magnolia, hawthorn, orchid tree.

Pacific Southwest & the Desert

Fertilize azaleas, camellias, summer-blooming bulbs, annuals, fuchsias, container plants, house plants. Feed fruit trees, vegetables.

Highlights. Late bulbs, annuals, and perennials; climbers: bougainvillea, honeysuckle; shrubs: rose, viburnum, weigela; trees: coral tree, citrus.

Pacific Northwest

Fertilize azaleas, camellias, rhododendrons, spring-blooming bulbs as they finish blooming, annuals, fuchsias, container plants, fruit trees, vegetables.

Highlights. Bulbs: anemone, ranuncula; early perennials; climbers: clematis, wisteria; shrubs: azalea, lilac, mock orange, mountain laurel, rhododendron, rose, viburnum; flowering trees.

Rocky Mountains & the Plains

Fertilize emerging perennials lightly. Apply pre-emergent weed killer to outdoor storage areas.

Highlights. Early bulbs: crocus, daffodil, grape hyacinth, species tulip; early perennials; shrubs: early azalea, flowering almond, forsythia, kerria, quince, viburnum, winter hazel; trees: Bradford pear, shadbush, star magnolia.

GARDEN MAINTENANCE

Northeast

Apply pre-emergent weed killer to outdoor storage areas. *Zone 6:* continue spring cleanup. Prepare beds for spring planting. Service irrigation systems. Begin hardening off annual seedlings. Begin rose care program. Lawn care: finish major work. *Zones 5, 4:* begin spring cleanup. Lawn care: begin major work (see March, Garden Maintenance, *zone 6*).

Mid-Atlantic

Complete removal of winter mulches. Prepare annual beds. Note gaps in bulb plantings and plan order for fall planting. Begin rose care program. Set stakes, poles, trellises. Begin moving annuals to cold frame to harden off. Apply pre-emergent weed killer to outdoor storage areas. Lawn care: finish major work.

Mid-South

Water and mulch newly planted and transplanted plants. Continue moving annual seedlings to cold frame to harden off. Turn compost pile. Begin weeding. Continue rose care program: deadhead, spray, fertilize, water. Begin moving house plants out for the summer. Lawn care: finish major work, fertilize cool- and warm-season grasses for second time.

Gulf & South Atlantic Coasts

Begin propagation by layering trees, shrubs, vines. Continue rose care program. Edge borders. Begin weeding, watering. Put fish out in lily ponds. Thin fruit trees. Stake, spray tomatoes. Lawn care: finish major cool-season lawn work, continue to plant warm-season grasses.

Pacific Southwest & the Desert

Begin propagation by layering trees, shrubs, vines. Continue rose care. Mulch new plantings. Edge beds, cultivate lightly, weed, water. Lawn care: *zone 9*—plant warm-season grasses (thatch Bermuda, St. Augustine grasses), seed or sod new lawns; *zones 8, 7*—mow, weed, feed, water established lawns.

Pacific Northwest

Continue rose care program. Begin propagation by layering established trees, shrubs, vines. Edge beds. Water, weed, lightly cultivate, and mulch beds. Set stakes. Add to and turn compost pile. Put fish out in lily ponds. Lawn care: mow, weed, water. *Zone 9:* move house plants outside as weather warms.

Rocky Mountains & the Plains

Continue spring cleanup. Mulch newly planted trees and shrubs, flower beds. Set stakes, poles, trellises. Edge beds and begin weeding. Thin vegetables. Compost garden cuttings unless diseased. Begin watering if season is dry. Put fish out in lily ponds. Lawn care: complete major lawn work.

Designing with Shrubs

Shrubs are selected primarily for their flowers during spring and summer, but because these seasons are of short duration, attention should be paid to their other decorative qualities—form, foliage, and texture—at other times of the year.

Shrubs are available in many different forms. Both form and growth habit should be considered before placing a shrub in your garden. Some species, such as yew *(Taxus),* come in weeping, spreading, columnar, and rounded varieties, but most species have only one naturally occurring form. Observe and respect it. Be aware of the mature shape and size of a plant and place it where it can develop naturally. Shrubs should not need annual pruning other than to remove dead, damaged, or crossing wood or to produce special effects. In formal gardens, shrubs can be pruned into topiaries, espaliers, and hedges. Hedges should always be pruned so that the top of the hedge is narrower than the bottom to allow light to the base and interior of the plant. Occasionally shrubs are limbed up into a tree form called a "standard." Once planted, shrubs require far less care than perennials.

Leaf drop will reveal more clearly the branching patterns, bark, buds, and thorns of deciduous shrubs. Japanese kerria, yellow- and red-twig dogwood, burning bush *(Euonymus alata),* devil's walking stick *(Aralia spinosa),* and oakleaf hydrangea *(Hydrangea quercifolia)* offer colorful or unusual bark. Seed heads and dried flowers remain on hydrangeas, clethra, althaea, enkianthus, and buddleia. Berries and fruits are persistent on cotoneaster, viburnum, holly, skimmia, sumac, and rosa rugosa. Blossom buds are prominent on pieris and shrub magnolias, and colorful thorns decorate many roses and hardy orange *(Poncirus trifoliata).*

Foliage is also important when selecting a shrub. It is an important design element because it is present in the garden before and after the flowers have faded. Foliage may vary in color according to the change of seasons.

Some shrubs, for instance purple-leaved smokebush *(Cotinus coggygria* var. 'Royal Purple') and some barberries *(Berberis* spp.), or the yellow-leaved elderberry *(Sambucus canadensis* var. 'Aurea'), golden spirea *(Spirea x bumalda),* and golden privet *(Ligustrum x vicayri),* are chosen for their colorful foliage. Other shrubs, including aucuba, euonymus, daphne, pittosporum, and some forms of shrub dogwoods, kerria, leucothoe, pieris, and weigela, have variegated leaves. Evergreen shrubs range in color from the rich greens of hollies and dwarf yew, to the gray- and blue-greens of junipers and rosemary, to the yellow-greens of dwarf false cypress *(Chamaecyparis* spp.). Including plants with colored foliage can relieve the monotony of too many dark green leaves.

Textures vary from the small, shiny leaves of Japanese holly or boxwood, to the prickly foliage of juniper, the coarse leaves of oakleaf hydrangea, the spears of yucca and phormium, to the compound leaflets of mahonia and the fanlike fronds of dwarf palms.

Shrubs grow naturally in the following forms:

- *Pyramidal* (most conifers, many holly species): use as free-standing or accent plants.
- *Columnar* (upright yews, Japanese hollies, arborvitae, pittosporum, buckthorn): use as accent plants in narrow places or as hedges.
- *Prostrate, spreading, or weeping* (rambling roses, cotoneaster, yews, jasmines, junipers, lowboy pyracantha): use

A single shrub can make a bold statement.

Shrubs with trailing branches add a sumptuous feel to the garden.

these horizontally growing shrubs to make excellent ground-cover plants on difficult slopes or banks, or as accent plants cascading over walls.

❧ *Compact, round-headed* (boxwood, yews, junipers, cherry or Grecian laurel, privet): use to add a civilized formal look as hedges, screening, and filler plants.

❧ *Mounding, fountainlike, cascading* (many deciduous spring- and summer-flowering shrubs—spireas, forsythias, roses, weigelas, buddleia): use to add a casual, natural look to an old-fashioned border, a mixed border, or informally in clumps on a hillside.

❧ *Upright, multistemmed* (lilacs, crape myrtle, privet, althaea, melaleuca): use these large shrubs, often trained to look like miniature trees, for emphasis in formal plantings or in containers.

When selecting shrubs for the garden, choose forms that suit the roles you want them to play. Plant evergreen hollies or yews as hedges to delineate spaces, edge a garden flower bed, create a boundary, or provide a private screen. Hide an unsightly air conditioner or ugly fence with a mass of dense, twiggy privet or lilac, not a row of upright evergreens, which might only underscore the problem. Use prostrate cotoneasters, junipers, or rambling roses as ground covers on banks and slopes that are difficult to mow and weed. Plant mounding shrubs in borders where their natural growth will be enhanced. Plant one variety in a group of three to five. They will grow together and look like a single large, handsome plant. Many different varieties jumbled together crowd each other out in visual competition, become spindly, and lose their potential charm.

In woodland areas, plant shade-tolerant species in sweeps and masses under trees. Shrubs in low-light areas grow upward, spreading and lifting their branches to catch enough sunlight. Combine dogwoods, azaleas, and rhododendrons, or ferns and fuchsias. Add bulbs and wildflowers to complete the natural look. In heavily shaded areas, limb up and thin out the tree canopy to allow as much light as possible to reach the ground.

Shrubs are also excellent candidates for container planting in handsome tubs to decorate an entrance or terrace. Evergreen hollies and laurel can be pruned into formal standards, and small-leafed plants such as Japanese holly into other topiary shapes. Shrubs that require special growing mediums can easily be catered to, and tender shrubs that require special care can be left outside in the summer and moved indoors in cool weather.

Select a few handsome shrubs for your garden. Choose them for their growth habits, ornamental qualities such as leaf textures and bark, fragrant blossoms, spring and fall foliage colors, fruits and persistent berries, and seedpods. To simplify and clarify any design, place shrubs wisely: repeat shapes, control the range of color, and plan according to the mature character of each. Shrubs create excitement, beauty, and color in the garden all year long.

CLIMBERS FOR ALL SEASONS

Climbing plants add a decorative, vertical element to the garden. They adorn walls and fences, outbuildings, trellises, and tree trunks. Requiring limited ground room, they grow upward and fill space not occupied by other plants. They cover surfaces with leaves in summer and create interesting patterns with their stems in winter.

Climbers are light-demanding plants accustomed to having cool, shaded roots—a reflection of their woodland origins. When trained on walls or other supports, they grow in length, not strength, sometimes attaching themselves, sometimes needing assistance. To determine how a vine can be used, it is important to know how it clings.

English ivy, euonymus, and climbing hydrangea have aerial rootlets, or holdfasts, that attach to roughened surfaces such as stone, brick, cement, or stucco. Virginia creeper has disks that secrete an adhesive resin, gluing it to roughened surfaces. These vines may grow heavy and need additional support, such as wires stretched horizontally at 5- to 7-foot intervals.

Clematis has tendrils—modified stems or sometimes leaf stalks—that twist around any nearby support, trellis, lattice, or wire fence to hold the plant in place. Wisteria and honeysuckle have twisting stems that easily twine around a wire or cord, a downspout, or a nearby tree trunk.

Plants with tendrils and twisting stems are not self-supporting. They need additional help if they are climbing anything but another plant. When training a wayward shoot, always follow the pattern of movement of the existing stem, rotating the shoot around the support in the same direction. Climbers are "preprogrammed." Bittersweet, akebia, and Chinese wisteria twist clockwise; Japanese honeysuckle, Japanese wisteria, and scarlet runner bean grow counterclockwise.

There are myriad annual and perennial vines, both evergreen and deciduous. Many other plants with elongated, arching stems, though they are not really vines, are considered climbers when they are trained against a flat surface. The best loved of these are climbing and rambling roses. Choose a climber as you would any other plant: for foliage, time of flowering, ornamental fruit, exposure hardiness, rate of growth, and ultimate size.

Northeast
Late frost is possible

Mid-Atlantic
Late frost is possible

Mid-South
Rising temperatures and rain probable

Gulf & South Atlantic Coasts
Rising temperatures and rain probable

Pacific Southwest & the Desert
Rising temperatures, dry weather

Pacific Northwest
Late frost is possible

Rocky Mountains & the Plains
Late frost is possible

GARDENING GUIDE ~ PLANTING

Northeast

Plant bare-root plants, evergreens, container-grown trees and shrubs, ground covers, perennials, annuals, summer-flowering bulbs, tropical water lilies, container plants when danger of frost is past. Divide crowded early bulbs and perennials. Sow warm-season vegetables or transplant with protection.

Mid-Atlantic

Plant container-grown trees and shrubs, ground covers, roses, perennials, containers, annuals, tropical water lilies when danger of frost is past. Divide crowded early spring-blooming perennials and bulbs. Transplant summer-blooming bulbs potted up in April. Sow and transplant warm-season vegetable seedlings.

Mid-South

Complete permanent spring plantings. Continue planting warm-season annuals, containers, tropical water lilies. Continue to dig and plant perennials. Plant annuals, daylilies, hosta, grasses in bulb beds to cover yellowing bulb foliage. Sow or transplant cool- and warm-season vegetables.

Gulf & South Atlantic Coasts

Complete spring planting and transplanting, planting of summer-flowering annuals and bulbs. Plant avocados, citrus. Continue planting summer- and fall-blooming perennials. Dig and divide tulip bulbs. Compost or store for replanting in the fall. Sow warm-season vegetables. Repot and prune house plants.

Pacific Southwest & the Desert

Plant container-grown trees and shrubs, tropicals. Plant avocados, citrus. Continue planting perennials. Pot up and set rooted chrysanthemum cuttings in the garden. Sow warm-season vegetables and herbs. *Zone 7:* continue planting warm-season annuals.

Pacific Northwest

Continue to plant container-grown trees and shrubs, perennials, vines. Set out summer-flowering bulbs. Divide overgrown summer- and fall-blooming perennials. Plant or sow warm-season vegetables and herbs. *Zone 8:* begin planting summer-blooming annuals, tropical water lilies.

Rocky Mountains & the Plains

Plant bare-root plants, evergreens, container-grown trees and shrubs, ground covers, perennials, annuals, containers when danger of frost is past. Divide crowded early spring-blooming perennials and bulbs. Set out summer-blooming bulbs. Sow wildflower seed. *Zone 6:* transplant with protection or sow warm-season vegetables.

PRUNING

Northeast

Complete pruning of winter-damaged trees and shrubs. Prune needle evergreens putting out new growth as needed. Continue to deadhead early spring-flowering bulbs, early annuals and perennials to promote rebloom.

Mid-Atlantic

Prune needle evergreens putting out new growth as needed. Prune spring-flowering trees and shrubs, wisteria as they finish blooming. Continue deadheading bulbs, early perennials, annuals to promote rebloom. Pinch back asters and chrysanthemums to delay bloom and thicken plants.

Mid-South

Prune needle evergreens as new foliage appears, hedges, and spring-flowering trees, shrubs, and vines as they finish blooming. Pinch back asters and chrysanthemums to thicken plants. Deadhead annuals to encourage rebloom. Take softwood cuttings and layer established plants to increase plant stock.

Gulf & South Atlantic Coasts

Complete pruning of late spring-blooming plants. Prune palms, tropical and subtropical plants, needle evergreens, hedges. Prune climbing roses after bloom. Pinch back chrysanthemums, asters, dahlias to produce compact plants. Cut back annuals, perennials, shrub roses to promote rebloom.

Pacific Southwest & the Desert

Prune climbing roses as they finish blooming. Complete pruning and deadheading of late spring-blooming plants. Prune azaleas lightly. Trim evergreens. Pinch back fall-blooming perennials. Deadhead fuchsias. Train espaliers, topiaries, bonsai. Take soft- and hardwood cuttings to increase stock.

Pacific Northwest

Prune climbing roses as they finish blooming. Complete pruning and deadheading of late spring-blooming plants. Prune needle evergreens as new growth appears. Pinch back fall-blooming perennials to delay bloom. Prune and shear annuals, perennials lightly. Prune palm and other tropical house plants.

Rocky Mountains & the Plains

Complete pruning of winter-damaged trees and shrubs, needle evergreens showing signs of new growth as needed. Pinch back chrysanthemums, asters to produce compact plants and delay bloom. Deadhead bulbs, perennials, annuals.

FERTILIZING & GARDEN HIGHLIGHTS

Northeast

Fertilize needle evergreens. Feed annuals and container plants, bulbs as they finish blooming.

> *Highlights.* Bulbs: fritillaria, lily of the valley, tulip, wood hyacinth; spring-blooming perennials, climbers, and shrubs; trees: redbud, saucer magnolia.

Mid-Atlantic

Fertilize perennials, annuals, house plants, bulbs.

> *Highlights.* Bulbs: allium, anemone, Dutch crocus, fritillaria, hyacinth, species tulip; perennials; spring-flowering shrubs; trees: magnolia, ornamental fruit trees.

Mid-South

Fertilize azaleas, bulbs, annuals, containers, fig trees every ten days.

> *Highlights.* Bulbs: calla lily, tulip; summer-blooming annuals and perennials; climbers: clematis, jasmine, wisteria; early summer-flowering shrubs; trees: evergreen and sweet bay magnolia, golden chain tree, stewartia, styrax, yellowwood.

Gulf & South Atlantic Coasts

Fertilize azaleas, camellias for second time, annuals, container plants, grapes, figs, vegetables.

> *Highlights.* Summer-blooming bulbs, annuals, perennials, and climbers; shrubs: late azalea, gardenia, hibiscus, hydrangea, oleander, plumbago, roses, vitex, yucca; trees: cassia, jacaranda, magnolia, mimosa, silk oak.

Pacific Southwest & the Desert

Fertilize azaleas, camellias, rhododendrons as they finish blooming, annuals, perennials, fuchsias, container plants, vegetables, grapes, newly planted citrus.

> *Highlights.* Summer-blooming bulbs, annuals, perennials, and climbers; shrubs: abelia, late azalea, deutzia, gardenia, hibiscus, hydrangea, lantana, lilac; trees: horse chestnut, jacaranda, Portugal laurel, locust.

Pacific Northwest

Fertilize azaleas, camellias, rhododendrons, bulbs, annuals, container plants.

> *Highlights.* Bulbs: daffodil, grape hyacinth; early perennials; shrubs: forsythia, pieris, spirea, spring heather, viburnum; trees: peach, plum, star magnolia.

Rocky Mountains & the Plains

Fertilize needle evergreens, annuals, container plants, house plants, bulbs as they finish blooming.

> *Highlights.* Spring-flowering bulbs and perennials; shrubs: currant, elderberry, honeysuckle, lilac, peashrub, quince, rose, shadbush, spirea, viburnum; trees: fruit trees, mountain ash.

GARDEN MAINTENANCE

Northeast

Continue spring cleanup. Mulch and edge newly planted beds. Set stakes, poles, trellises. Begin weeding. Thin vegetables. Begin watering if season is dry. Put fish out in lily ponds. Begin moving cool-temperature house plants outdoors for the summer. Lawn care: *zones 5, 4*—finish major work; fertilize cool-season grasses for second time.

Mid-Atlantic

Mulch trees, shrubs, flower beds. Edge borders, begin weeding. Set stakes, poles, trellises. Begin watering if season is dry. Continue rose care program. Move cool-temperature, tropical house plants outdoors for the summer. Lawn care: fertilize cool-season grasses for second time; set mower at 2 1/2"–3", mow regularly.

Mid-South

Mulch newly planted and established trees and shrubs, small plants. Continue summer maintenance. Put fish out in lily ponds. Thin heavily laden fruit trees. Move house plants outdoors for the summer. Lawn care: seed, plug, or sod warm-season grasses, fertilize monthly, keep well watered.

Gulf & South Atlantic Coasts

Remulch beds to 2"–4". Continue rose care. Cultivate annual beds lightly. Weed when soil is damp—it is easier. Pull spent vegetables. Add to and turn compost pile. Begin cutting herbs, flowers for drying. Lawn care: start new warm-season lawns or overseed established ones, fertilize monthly, mow and water regularly.

Pacific Southwest & the Desert

Remulch beds. Continue rose care. Dig and compost spent tulip and hyacinth bulbs, spent vegetables. Net berries. Weed when soil is damp—it is easier. Lawn care: fertilize warm-season grasses monthly, set mower at 1"—mow and leave clippings on lawn from now until fall, water regularly and deeply, apply weed killer if necessary.

Pacific Northwest

Pull spent spring-blooming annuals and compost. Water and weed regularly. Keep beds edged and mulched. Set stakes, poles, trellises. Add to and turn compost pile. Continue rose care. Lawn care: fertilize warm-season grasses monthly, water and mow regularly.

Rocky Mountains & the Plains

Continue spring cleanup, lawn work. Mulch trees, shrubs, flower beds, berry bushes, vegetables. Edge borders. Set stakes, poles, trellises. Begin weeding, watering. Thin vegetables. Continue rose care. Compost garden cuttings unless diseased. Put fish out in lily ponds. Lawn care: fertilize cool-season grasses for second time, water and mow regularly.

DESIGNING WITH CLIMBERS AND WALL PLANTS

Gardens offer many opportunities to use climbing plants to add greenery and color to vertical spaces.

For pure sheets of color, no vine can compete with the clematis species. Cut blossoms last as long as ten days in arrangements and many have decorative and unusual seed heads. Blooming times of different species vary from late spring until frost. Clematis and other deciduous vines climbing with tendrils can be trained on trellises or posts, or allowed to climb up into trees and shrubs.

Climbing and rambling roses are tall (6–20 feet), natural mutations or "sports" of any one of the other rose types. They can be treated as climbers or wall plants and trained against a wall or pillar. In the wild, thorns act as tendrils, and roses manage to clamp onto and work themselves up into trees. Climbing roses put out long, thorny shoots that without help eventually topple over and build up into huge tangled masses. Pillar roses have stiff, upright stems. Climbing roses have pliable ones, and with encouragement from screw eyes and twine, can scale trees or decorate arches and fences. Rambling roses have weak, trailing stems. They can cascade over walls or sprawl out as ground covers.

Vines trained on arbors, or on posts with wires stretched between them, become man-made trees shading outdoor living spaces. When a vine is spread out over a large surface, the maximum amount of flowering wood is exposed to the sun and the vine produces a rich display of leaves and flowers. Grapevines on pergolas and arbors are a classic. They provide cool shade, rich fall color, and an edible fruit crop. In a hot climate, Queen's wreath (*Antigonon leptopus*) will provide rapid shade for people and sun-sensitive plants.

Vines can decorate plain wall surfaces, hide or disguise ugly views, and give protection from the wind. Once established, perennial vines, including actinidia, trumpet vine, silver lace, and fleece vine, will provide permanent coverage within a year. For bold texture as well as screening, try smooth Dutchman's pipe (*Aristolochia macrophylla*). Foliage vines with fragrant flowers include Dutch honeysuckle (*Lonicera periclymenum*), trumpet honeysuckle (*L. sempervirens*), and silver vine (*Actinidia polygama*). Annual vines such as mandevilla, morning glory, moonflower, and scarlet runner bean will give coverage and blossoms for a season.

Low walls and balustrades are good places for well-trimmed, low-growing, or miniature vines such as Kenilworth ivy (*Cymbalaria muralis*), an annual in cold climates, baby wintercreeper (*Euonymus fortunei* var. 'Minima'), or Low's ivy (*Parthenocissus tricuspidata* var. 'Lowii'). Use baby wintercreeper at the base of a small statue or urn. Plant Low's ivy to spill over a low wall or soften stone steps.

In the wild garden, let a sweet autumn clematis (*C. paniculata*), climbing hydrangea (*H. petiolaris*), or bittersweet (*Celastrus scandens*) scramble over rocks and fallen logs, or let a small flowering clematis wander through ferns and wildflowers.

Grow a vine in a container or hanging basket, or in an urn placed on a pedestal. Try Japanese hop (*Humulus* spp.), an annual, to give rapid coverage and provide contrast to finer foliage plants. Place a small trellis in a container to support a black-eyed Susan vine. Plant glory vine (*Eccremocarpus scaber*), an annual in the North, in a hanging basket or large container to show off its long, orange-scarlet blooms. Grow tender vines, bignonia, and jasmine in cool climates in containers that can be moved indoors for shelter in winter, or in any climate for quick vertical color and background. Shade the interior of the greenhouse with hyacinth bean (*Dolichos lablab*). Add spring color in the vegetable garden with sweet peas trained on strings, or grow vining vegetables—cucumbers, melons, New Zealand spinach, peas, pole beans, squash, tomatoes—on trellises to save space and add a background for other plants. Add height to a flower border by growing a climbing rose on a tripod amidst low shrubs or perennials.

Difficult and unmowable banks can be covered with rapidly growing and attractive rambling roses, ivy, or honeysuckle to ease maintenance and control erosion; chain-link fences can be hidden under sweet autumn clematis; an ugly tree stump can be disguised with a perennial pea vine (*Lathyrus* spp.).

Many rampant vines and wall shrubs become bare at the bottom as they develop. Some supports may need hiding. Underplant a tall vine or naked lower trunks with a lower shrub that blooms on a different schedule.

Vines need occasional pruning. Thinning and trimming are important to keep them within bounds. To enhance their appearance they can be tailored to expose branching structure and silhouette individual leaves. Rapidly growing vines such as wisteria should be kept under control. They can grow 20 feet or more in a year and become a nuisance, traveling into gutters and windows and growing under roof tiles. They can be allowed to grow up a tree trunk so long as they do not mask the leaves, which would weaken the tree.

Many shrubs may be treated as wall plants and grown to fit spaces between windows as well as to fit the height of a wall. Well trained and well pruned, a wall shrub may provide a more interesting and colorful display of foliage and flowers than a vine. In addition the wall will give a tender shrub the extra warmth and protection it needs to survive. Shrubs such as abutilon, bougainvillea, ceanothus, and sasanqua camellia, where hardy, as well as forsythia, weeping cotoneaster, winter jasmine, viburnum, Japanese maple, and magnolia can be used.

Espaliering is a more formal method of shaping and controlling plants to limit them to one plane. Espaliering is an art form that shows all the finer details of its subject: the line of the trunk and branches and the texture of the bark. Shrubs and small trees that normally grow in the round can be pruned to two dimensions. They will have height and width, but no depth. Espaliered plants can be designed in various formal patterns. In a winter garden, plants frequently espaliered are fruit trees, pyracantha, hollies, evergreen magnolia, junipers, blue atlas cedar, and yew.

Bougainvillea and cat relaxing on a garden wall.

Rose arbors never fail to delight.

PERENNIALS FOR ALL SEASONS

Perennial plants, in formal and mixed borders, in island beds, in containers and hanging baskets, satisfy our craving for color. These flowers, which originated in wild meadows, in forests, and on streamsides, have been domesticated and transformed by plant hybridizers into hardy garden favorites. Perennials provide waves of color and seasonal change from early spring to late autumn. At the end of the growing season, stems, seed heads, and blossom heads can be left standing to dry, adding interest to winter landscapes.

Perennials are defined as herbaceous plants that live and flower for three or more years where climate and gardening conditions are favorable. Their leafy tops die back to the ground each winter, sometimes leaving a rosette of leaves. Their roots live on underground. Perennial is a relative term. In warm climates many perennials, such as primroses, violas, and Iceland poppies, that do not tolerate excessive heat are treated as annuals and set out each year. In northern gardens many tender perennials are used as annual bedding and container plants.

Intense use of perennials began in the late nineteenth century with William Robinson and Gertrude Jekyll, who designed gardens on a large scale. They featured perennials in long, deep beds at the edge of formal lawns or in informal cottage gardens. Plants were carefully placed by height and color and backed by clipped evergreen hedges or high walls. Often the borders featured either one color or a rainbowlike wave of mixed colors. "Filler" plants—other perennials, annuals, or bulbs—were grown in greenhouses and rotated in and out of the borders to provide maximum color and prevent any gaps among the garden's blooms. This practice required a tremendous amount of labor: constantly lifting and dividing, staking, deadheading, fertilizing, and watering to keep the plants vigorous.

Claude Monet at Giverny in the 1900s, Lawrence Johnson at Hidecote in the 1920s, and Vita Sackville-West at Sissinghurst Castle in the 1930s experimented with using perennials more informally. Today's designers of modern gardens have freed perennials to be used in endless ways that display their natural charms: in mixed plantings with trees, shrubs, bulbs, and ornamental grasses; in formal and informal borders; in island beds; and in meadow, bog, and water plantings.

Perennials, a versatile and rewarding group of plants, are easy to grow, and can be moved about in bloom for instant color design experiments. They can also be divided to increase stock and still be counted on to return faithfully year after year.

Northeast
Summer weather conditions prevail

Mid-Atlantic
Summer weather conditions prevail

Mid-South
Summer weather conditions prevail

Gulf & South Atlantic Coasts
Summer weather conditions prevail

Pacific Southwest & the Desert
Summer weather conditions prevail

Pacific Northwest
Summer weather conditions prevail

Rocky Mountains & the Plains
Summer weather conditions prevail

GARDENING GUIDE ~ PLANTING

Northeast

Plant container-grown trees, shrubs, ground covers, annuals, cannas, gladiolus. Transplant roses, perennials. Divide late spring-blooming bulbs. Start annuals in flats to cover later-summer bare spots. Sow and transplant seedlings of warm-season vegetables and herbs.

Mid-Atlantic

Plant container-grown trees and shrubs, ground covers, perennials. Divide late spring-blooming bulbs. Plant cannas and gladiolus, fast-growing annuals. Transplant evergreens, roses, perennials. Sow warm-season vegetables in the garden. Sow cabbage family and Brussels sprouts in flats for fall crops.

Mid-South

Complete permanent plantings. Transplant roses, perennials. Plant summer- and fall-blooming lilies, bulbs, gladiolus for fall bloom. Dig and store tulip bulbs for fall planting. Sow fast-growing summer- and fall-blooming annuals in bare spots. Sow warm-season vegetables for a fall crop.

Gulf & South Atlantic Coasts

Plant cold-hardy palms. Plant warm-season annuals in bare spots. Transplant roses, perennials. *Zone 10:* sow tropical vegetables. *Zones 10, 9:* sow warm-season vegetables.

Pacific Southwest & the Desert

Continue to plant warm-season annuals in bare spots and containers. Continue to divide and rejuvenate early perennials. Sow and transplant warm-season vegetables. *Zones 10, 9:* complete permanent plantings until cooler weather in fall.

Pacific Northwest

Plant container-grown plants. Complete permanent plantings. Continue planting warm-season annuals, summer- and fall-blooming bulbs. Continue to divide and rejuvenate early summer-blooming perennials. Sow or transplant warm-season vegetables.

Rocky Mountains & the Plains

Plant container-grown trees and shrubs, ground covers, annuals, cannas, gladiolus. Start annuals for late-summer color. Transplant roses, perennials. Divide crowded late-spring bulbs and perennials. Sow or set out seedlings of warm-season vegetables and herbs.

year _____

year _____

PRUNING

Northeast

Prune deciduous and evergreen hedges, spring-flowering trees and shrubs, wisteria after bloom. Remove dead and diseased wood and water sprouts from dogwoods. Pinch back asters, chrysanthemums. Deadhead rhododendron, laurel, lilac, perennials, annual herbs. Take softwood cuttings to increase plant stock.

Mid-Atlantic

Prune deciduous and evergreen hedges, spring-flowering trees and shrubs after bloom. Remove dead and diseased wood and water sprouts from dogwoods. Pinch back asters, chrysanthemums. Deadhead annuals, perennials. Take softwood cuttings to increase plant stock. Cut raspberry canes to the ground after fruiting.

Mid-South

Prune hedges; cut narrower at top than bottom to allow light to reach lower branches. Pinch back chrysanthemums to retard bloom and thicken plants. Deadhead annuals, perennials, spring-blooming shrubs. Cut raspberry canes to the ground when they finish fruiting.

Gulf & South Atlantic Coasts

Prune deadwood, weak or diseased branches on large trees and shrubs to protect from hurricane damage. Prune palms and other tropical and subtropical plants. Trim hedges as necessary. Pinch back annuals, herbs, chrysanthemums, poinsettias. Deadhead perennials. Take softwood cuttings and layer established plants to increase stock.

Pacific Southwest & the Desert

Prune vines, suckers, deadwood, and weak or diseased branches from large trees to prevent storm damage. Pinch back fall-blooming perennials to delay bloom. Deadhead perennials. Allow favorites to reseed themselves. Cut all blackberry canes that have finished fruiting to the ground.

Pacific Northwest

Prune vines, deadwood, and weak or diseased branches from large trees to protect from storm damage. Deadhead perennials. Allow favorites to reseed themselves. Pinch back fall asters and chrysanthemums to delay bloom and thicken plants.

Rocky Mountains & the Plains

Prune deciduous and evergreen hedges, spring-flowering trees and shrubs, wisteria after bloom. Remove dead and diseased wood and water sprouts from plants. Pinch back chrysanthemums and asters to delay bloom and thicken plants. Deadhead lilacs. Take softwood cuttings to increase plant stock.

year _____

FERTILIZING & GARDEN HIGHLIGHTS

Northeast

Fertilize acid-loving, flowering evergreens after bloom, annuals, container plants, house plants monthly.

Highlights. Bulbs: allium, lilies; annuals and perennials; climbers: climbing hydrangea, moonflower, morning glory; early summer-flowering shrubs and trees.

Mid-Atlantic

Fertilize broadleaf evergreens. Feed annuals, container plants, house plants monthly. Fertilize vegetables, including asparagus.

Highlights. Height of early-summer bloom.

Mid-South

Fertilize evergreens, deciduous trees and shrubs, ground covers, annuals, containers, house plants summering outside, vegetables.

Highlights. Summer-blooming bulbs, annuals, perennials, flowering vines, roses, shrubs, and trees.

Gulf & South Atlantic Coasts

Fertilize annuals, chrysanthemums, container plants, vegetables, house plants. Feed tropical palms.

Highlights. Summer-blooming annuals; perennials: daylilies, purple coneflower; shrubs: althaea, gardenia, hibiscus, hydrangea, lantana, oleander, plumbago, rose; trees: crape myrtle, mimosa.

Pacific Southwest & the Desert

Fertilize annuals, container plants, house plants, chrysanthemums, citrus, tropicals, subtropicals. Feed azaleas, camellias. Spray poison oak and ivy.

Highlights. Summer-blooming bulbs and annuals; shrubs: bottlebush, fuchsia, gardenia, hibiscus, hydrangea, mock orange, oleander, spirea, rose; trees: cape chestnut, goldenrain tree.

Pacific Northwest

Fertilize permanent plantings, annuals, container plants, chrysanthemums, house plants summering outside, herbs, vegetables, berry bushes.

Highlights. Summer-blooming annuals, perennials, and flowering vines; shrubs: choisya, deutzia, escallonia, hydrangea, hypericum, potentilla, rose, smokebush; trees: sweetbay magnolia.

Rocky Mountains & the Plains

Fertilize annuals, containers, house plants monthly. Fertilize vegetables with foliar spray.

Highlights. Summer-blooming bulbs, annuals, and perennials; climbers: clematis, goldflame honeysuckle, wisteria; shrubs: hydrangea, mock orange, nandina, potentilla, rose, spirea, viburnum; trees: catalpa, goldenrain tree, tree lilac.

GARDEN MAINTENANCE

Northeast

Continue rose care program. Set stakes, poles, trellises. Train plants. Water and weed. Thin vegetables. Place netting over berries to protect from birds. Be prepared to protect warm-season crops from late frosts in cold areas. Move tropical house plants outdoors. Lawn care: set mower at $2\frac{1}{2}"$–3", water thoroughly weekly.

Mid-Atlantic

Mulch perennial beds for summer. Set new plants through the mulch. Continue rose care program. Train plants growing on trellises. Thin vegetables, annual herbs. Water if season is dry. Weed when soil is damp—it is easier. Lawn care: set mower at $2\frac{1}{2}"$–3"; water thoroughly weekly.

Mid-South

Stake floppy plants. Weed. Add to compost pile. Begin cutting herbs, flowers for drying. Wash conifer foliage vigorously to dislodge insects. Water trees, shrubs by deep soaking. Mulch vegetables to control weeds, moisture loss. Lawn care: fertilize established warm-season lawns monthly; mow, water regularly.

Gulf & South Atlantic Coasts

Keep beds well mulched. Edge, weed beds. Stake floppy plants. Continue rose care program: deadhead, spray, fertilize. Continue cutting herbs, flowers for drying. Water trees, shrubs by deep soaking. Pull and compost spent vegetable crops. Lawn care: lightly feed warm-season grasses monthly.

Pacific Southwest & the Desert

Keep beds, trees, shrubs well weeded and mulched. Stake floppy plants. Spray conifer foliage vigorously with water to dislodge insects. Continue rose care program. Begin cutting flowers, herbs for drying. Water deeply. Lawn care: maintain established lawns at correct height; feed warm-season grasses lightly.

Pacific Northwest

Begin cutting herbs, flowers for drying. Continue to pull and compost spent annuals, vegetable crops. Stake floppy plants. Continue rose care program of deadheading, spraying, feeding. Spray conifer foliage vigorously to discourage insects, prevent diseases, and sunscald. Lawn care: feed new and established lawns.

Rocky Mountains & the Plains

Water thoroughly weekly. Stake and tie tall, floppy plants. Train plants growing on poles and trellises. Continue rose care program. Edge and weed beds. Add to and turn compost pile. Mulch to conserve moisture. Protect tender plants from late frost. Move tropical house plants outdoors to shaded areas. Lawn care: set mower to 2 1/2"–3".

DESIGNING WITH PERENNIALS

Recent years have seen an explosion of interest in perennials. An overwhelming number of new varieties and cultivars have appeared, as well as new ways found to use perennials in the garden. Before choosing perennials, determine if your site is sunny or shady, moist or dry, the soil acidic or alkaline. Most perennials are tolerant of a broad range of conditions, but will truly flourish only if their specific requirements are met. Conditions can be altered: trees can be limbed up and thinned if shade is too heavy, or shrubs and trees can be added to create shade. Drainage can be improved by amending the soil or planting in raised beds. Soil pH can be adjusted, within limits, by the addition of lime or sulfur. Whenever possible, however, it is better not to fight the existing conditions but to choose perennials that are at home in them. Turn a rocky outcropping into an alpine landscape, a wet spot into a bog for moisture-loving plants, an endless dry expanse of lawn into a meadow, a cluster of trees growing in acid soil into a woodland garden. Special sites offer opportunities to create a specific community of plants with similar cultural habits. As groups, these plants will harmonize in texture and color.

Classic formal perennial borders look best planted on level ground with a background of evergreen hedges, walls, or fences. The depth of the bed should be in proportion to the height of its background and at least one-third the height of the tallest plants within it. Be generous for greater impact. Leave space behind the border for a service path to ease maintenance and increase air circulation. In laying out the bed, use groups of plants, not individual ones—the smaller the actual plant, the greater the number of plants needed within the group. Use sweeps and masses to create a rhythm down the length of the border. Make changes in height from front to back, determining the position of the plant in the border by the height of the foliage, not of its blossoms. Outline individual areas on the soil with a sprinkling of lime and set stakes of different heights with colored ribbons on them to represent various groupings and help you visualize your design. Draw a plan and color in the plants by season of interest, making sure there is something blooming from spring to fall. Think of contrasting foliage colors, shapes, and textures as well as blossom color. Remember, a blossom lasts only a few weeks! Choose plants that have outstanding foliage before and after bloom: aloe, alchemilla, arum, bergenia, hosta, hellebore, heuchera, hardy geranium, iris, ligularia, phormium, rodgersia, and yucca, for example. They will be a great asset and contribute to a long-lasting picture.

Make an existing bed more interesting by widening it to make room for groupings of herbaceous perennials plants. Existing trees, shrubs, or hedges will provide a background to frame the perennials in summer and carry the shape of the garden in winter when they die down. Mixed borders provide windbreaks and shelter for tender plants and reduce the necessity for staking. A long season of interest results from planting a mixture of bulbs, perennials, and flowering and berrying shrubs and trees.

Perennials can also be set in free-form island beds designed to be walked around and viewed from all sides. Island beds do not require level ground and look best in a spacious garden. Set the scale of the bed to fit comfortably into the surrounding grassy area, preferably toward one side to avoid intruding on the principal sweep of the lawn. The bed should be twice as wide as the tallest plant is high. Use tall perennials—aruncus, asters, boltonia, macleaya, ornamental grasses, and globe thistle—for height and accent in the center, and contrast them with the rounded leaves of acanthus, hosta, phlomis, or rodgersia. Fill in the edges with low ground-cover plants like alchemilla, astilbe, candytuft, catmint, campanula, dianthus, heuchera, and stachys.

In meadows, sow or set out seedlings of perennials. Mix in annual seeds to give color the first year before the meadow is established. Using the same approach on a smaller scale, introduce a meadow into your garden. Use plants native to your region and suited to your weather conditions. Reduce an extended area of grass to create a transitional zone between formal lawn and woodland, hillside, or canyon, or near the water. Add a fence with a gate and mow a path through the meadow to make it more inviting.

To any perennial garden, add summer- and fall-blooming bulbs (allium, babiana, belamcanda, camassia, colchicum, crocosmia, gladiolus, ixia, hardy lilies, lycoris, nerine, watsonia) to push up through the early-blooming perennials that fade.

Do not overlook perennials as problem solvers. On banks too difficult to mow, follow early spring-blooming bulbs with daylilies or black-eyed Susans. Brighten dark shady corners with astilbe, variegated hosta, and ferns. In hot dry courtyards, try drought-resistant herbs such as lavender, sage, and rosemary, or artemisia, thyme, and sedum.

Try container plantings of perennials in outdoor spaces—on roof gardens and decks, on patios and terraces, in small courtyards and flanking entrances. Pick a container that will not overwhelm the plant and that blends with the color, texture, and architectural style of the background. Containers are especially useful for dealing with tender plants because they can be moved indoors for protection when necessary. Ornamental grasses, herbs, and sedum show off well in containers, as do yucca and marguerites. Fuchsias, daylilies, scented geraniums, phormium, and many other herbs, succulents, and bulbs are only a few of the possibilities.

Consider the following perennials for specific sites and to lengthen the season.

PARTIAL SHADE: anemone, bellflower, bluebells, brunnera, cardinal flower, celandine poppy, cimicifuga, columbine, corydalis, epimedium, foamflower, foxglove, wild ginger, hellebore, crested iris, Jacob's ladder, lamium, blue phlox, primroses, pulmonaria, trillium, violets.

DRY SHADE: acanthus, alchemilla, brunnera, epimedium, euphorbia, geranium, lamium, liriope, polygonum, stachys, tiarella.

DAMP SITES: aruncus, astilbe, brunnera, cardinal flower, chelone, eupatorium (Joe-Pye weed), hibiscus, hosta, ferns, filipendula, moisture-loving grasses (acorus, arundo, carex), gunnera, Siberian iris, marsh marigold, monarda, myosotis, peltiphyllum, Japanese primula, rodgersia, thalictrum, tradescantia, trollius, violets.

WET SITES: amsonia, cattails, flag iris, lobelia, swamp sunflower, water lily.

DROUGHT-RESISTANT (full sun): achillea, artemisia, asclepias, aster, baptisia, centaurea, coreopsis, dianthus (some), echinops, eryngium, gaillardia, scented geranium, goldenrod, helianthemum, hemerocallis, lavender, perovskia, phlomis, plumbago, rudbeckia, salvia, santolina, sedums, stachys, thyme, verbena, yucca (not a true perennial but frequently included as one).

LONG-LIVED: achillea, aconitum, amsonia, anemone, artemisia, asclepias, astilbe, baptisia, boltonia, campanula, coreopsis, dicentra, dictamnus, doronicum, echinacea, echinops, euphorbia, filipendula, gaillardia, geranium, hemerocallis, hosta, iris, peony, platycodon, polygonatum, rudbeckia, saponaria, thalictrum, tradescantia, veronica, yucca.

EARLY SPRING: adonis, arabis, armeria, aubrieta, bergenia, brunnera, claytonia, dicentra, euphorbia, hellebore, marsh marigold, phlox, primula, pulmonaria.

LATE FALL: fall anemone, asters, hardy begonia, chrysanthemums, Montauk daisy, goldenrod, boltonia, ornamental grasses, patrinia, perovskia, rudbeckia, sedums, tricyrtis.

A magnificent perennial border with warm summer colors.

ANNUALS FOR ALL SEASONS

An annual is a plant that completes its life cycle in a single growing season. Most annuals will flower six to ten weeks after their seed is sown; many stay in bloom for months. In warm climates, annuals will stay in bloom the whole year if they are given good care and the spent blossoms are removed regularly. Eventually, all annuals produce seed and die.

A biennial is a two-year annual. Sown from seed in the summer, biennials such as pansies, foxglove, and sweet William produce a rosette of leaves before fall. The following spring, a flower stalk will rise to bloom and make seed. To save garden space, biennials are usually sown in the vegetable garden or cold frame, to be transplanted to their blooming positions in the garden the following spring. Because biennials, like annuals, will reseed themselves with uncertain results, they are sown and transplanted annually.

There are three major classifications of annuals, which describe their response to frost: hardy, half-hardy, and tender.

Hardy annuals (calendula, pansies, stock) germinate at low temperatures and withstand light frost in the spring and fall. They are usually sown directly in the garden, in the spot where they will flower, as soon as the soil is friable. A few are super-hardy (forget-me-nots, larkspur, nigella, poppies, sweet peas); they can be sown in late fall to germinate and then spend the winter as small seedlings. Hardy annual seed can be spread on late-winter snows for early spring germination.

Half-hardy annuals (erinus, euphorbia, four-o'clocks, kochia, lobelia, nicotiana) will survive some light frost but are usually planted in the open around the last frost date or slightly later.

Tender annuals (impatiens, marigolds, petunias) cannot withstand any frost at all. They need warm weather and soil to germinate and flourish. In warm climates many tender annuals are sown directly into the ground. In cooler climates they are started indoors in flats or in the greenhouse, or bought in flats as seedlings at garden centers to be transplanted outside once the weather warms up. Homegrown ones will need to be "hardened off."

Our contemporary use of annuals is a simplified successor to the Victorian passion for "bedding out." Victorian gardeners set out large numbers of brightly colored, hothouse-grown tropical seedlings each year in formal and intricate geometric patterns, a process that was overwhelmingly labor-intensive. In the relatively maintenance-free garden of today, annuals planted informally lend themselves to temporary, brilliant effects quickly, easily, and inexpensively.

Northeast
Hot weather prevails

Mid-Atlantic
Hot weather prevails

Mid-South
Hot, humid weather prevails

Gulf & South Atlantic Coasts
Hot, humid weather prevails

Pacific Southwest & the Desert
Hot, dry weather prevails

Pacific Northwest
Hot weather

Rocky Mountains & the Plains
Hot, dry weather prevails

Sappiglosis in bloom.

91

GARDENING GUIDE ~ PLANTING

Northeast

Continue planting container-grown trees and shrubs, perennials, annuals. Sow biennials in flats or nursery beds. Divide and rejuvenate iris, poppies, crowded bulbs. Sow warm- and cool-season vegetables in the garden for a fall crop.

Mid-Atlantic

Continue to plant container-grown trees and shrubs, perennials, annuals. Sow biennials in flats or nursery beds. Divide crowded iris, poppies. Sow warm- and cool-season vegetables for a fall crop.

Mid-South

Start perennials, cool-season biennials in flats or nursery beds. Divide and rejuvenate crowded spring-blooming perennials. Plant summer-flowering bedding plants in bare areas. Start fall vegetable crops, including cabbage family and collard greens, in flats. Set out fall tomato plants, garlic cloves to winter over.

Gulf & South Atlantic Coasts

INDOORS—Sow fast-growing annuals, including vines, for fall bloom in bare spots. Continue to plant summer-flowering bedding plants. Sow seeds for spring wildflower meadows. Dig and divide spring-blooming perennials. *Zone 9:* start cool-season vegetables for a fall crop.

Pacific Southwest & the Desert

Continue to sow fast-growing, fall-blooming annuals. Sow seeds or set seedlings of California natives for spring wildflower meadows and drought-resistant gardens. Divide and rejuvenate spring-blooming perennials. Plant summer- and fall-bloomers. *Zone 8:* start cool-season annuals and vegetables for fall planting in the garden.

Pacific Northwest

Divide and rejuvenate spring-blooming perennials. Sow cool-season biennials, perennials in flats or nursery beds to transplant to the garden in spring. Continue planting summer-blooming annuals. Transplant cool-season vegetable seedlings to the garden. Dig shallots.

Rocky Mountains & the Plains

Continue planting container-grown trees and shrubs, perennials, annuals. Start biennials in flats or nursery beds. Sow or transplant cool- and warm-season vegetables to the garden. Divide and transplant iris, poppies, crowded bulbs.

year _____

PRUNING

year _____

Northeast

Prune and thin major shade trees to allow more light on thin lawns. Prune shrub and perennial borders, deciduous and evergreen hedges, climbing roses after bloom. Pinch asters and chrysanthemums for last time. Shear annuals lightly. Cut spent raspberry canes to the ground. Take softwood cuttings.

Mid-Atlantic

Prune and thin major shade trees to allow more light on thin lawns. Prune shrub and perennial borders. Prune climbing and rambler roses, azaleas, rhododendrons after bloom. Deadhead perennials. Pinch back asters and chrysanthemums for last time. Shear annuals lightly. Take ground-cover, house-plant cuttings.

Mid-South

Continue pruning late-blooming trees and shrubs as necessary. Prune climbing and rambler roses after bloom. Cut withered fern fronds to the ground. Pinch back chrysanthemums. Shear and deadhead annuals to prolong bloom. Cut back woody herbs. Take softwood cuttings to increase stock.

Gulf & South Atlantic Coasts

Prune wisteria for last time. Shear back annuals, perennials, and deadhead crape myrtles to encourage rebloom. Pinch back chrysanthemums, dahlias, poinsettias. Cut back woody herbs. Cut withered fern fronds, aspidistra to the ground.

Pacific Southwest & the Desert

Prune wisteria for last time. Trim hedges lightly. Shear back annuals, fuchsias, perennials. Keep pinching back chrysanthemums, dahlias. Cut withered fern fronds to the ground to promote new growth. Prune citrus. Thin overladen fruit crops to prevent damage to limbs. Take softwood cuttings.

Pacific Northwest

Prune wisteria for last time. Prune late-blooming trees and shrubs, rambler and climbing roses. Keep pinching back chrysanthemums, dahlias. Cut back woody herbs. Thin heavily laden fruit trees to prevent damage to limbs. Take softwood cuttings, including herbs, to increase plant stock.

Rocky Mountains & the Plains

Prune shrub and perennial beds and thin major shade trees to allow more light to lawns and lessen possibility of storm damage. Trim deciduous and evergreen hedges. Prune climbing and rambler roses after bloom. Pinch back asters and chrysanthemums. Shear annuals lightly. Take softwood cuttings.

year _____

year _____

FERTILIZING & GARDEN HIGHLIGHTS

Northeast

Fertilize fall-blooming perennials, annuals, container plants, house plants.

> *Highlights.* Summer-blooming annuals, perennials, and vines; shrubs: abelia, althaea, butterfly bush, clethra, oakleaf hydrangea, hypericum, rose, viburnum; trees: stewartia.

Mid-Atlantic

Fertilize broadleaf evergreens, annuals, container plants, house plants, vegetables. Spray unwanted weeds and grass in paved areas with systemic herbicide.

> *Highlights.* Summer-blooming annuals, perennials, shrubs, and vines, trees: crape myrtle, sophora, sourwood, stewartia.

Mid-South

Fertilize annuals, container plants, house plants, chrysanthemums, vegetables, languishing herbs. Spray poison ivy with systemic herbicide.

> *Highlights.* Summer-blooming bulbs, annuals, and perennials; shrubs: althaea, bottlebush, buckeye, butterfly bush, clethra, gardenia, hibiscus, hypericum; trees: crape myrtle.

Gulf & South Atlantic Coasts

Fertilize annuals, container plants, house plants, chrysanthemums, vegetable seedlings.

> *Highlights.* Summer-blooming bulbs: begonia, caladium, gladiolus, montbretia, tuberose; summer-blooming annuals; perennials, including water lilies; summer-flowering shrubs and vines; trees: crape myrtle.

Pacific Southwest & the Desert

Fertilize annuals, container plants, house plants, gardenias, chrysanthemums, established citrus.

> *Highlights.* Summer-blooming bulbs, annuals, and perennials; climbers: bougainvillea, coral vine, trumpet vine; summer-flowering shrubs; trees: cassia, silk tree.

Pacific Northwest

Fertilize annuals, container plants, house plants, fall-blooming perennials. Apply milorganite to lawns.

> *Highlights.* Bulbs: begonia, gladiolus, tritoma; annuals and perennials; shrubs: abelia, butterfly bush, ceanothus, clethra, escallonia, fuchsia, spirea, tamarisk; trees: sophora, sourwood.

Rocky Mountains & the Plains

Fertilize annuals, container plants, house plants, chrysanthemums. Feed vegetables, rhubarb, asparagus after last harvest.

> *Highlights.* Annuals; perennials; climbers: clematis, climbing hydrangea, morning glory, moonflower, trumpet vine, scarlet runner bean; shrubs.

Garden Maintenance

Northeast

Cut herbs, flowers for drying. Stake tall plants. Water and weed. Cultivate plant beds lightly to reduce compaction and weeds. Pull spent annuals, vegetables. Add to and turn compost pile. Place orders for fall planting. Lawn care: maintain grass at 3"; water weekly if needed.

Mid-Atlantic

Begin cutting flowers, herbs for drying. Stake and tie plants. Cultivate beds lightly to reduce compaction and weeds. Remulch beds if necessary. Water deeply. Pull and replace spent vegetable crops with early-maturing varieties. Lawn care: maintain grass at 3"; water weekly if necessary.

Mid-South

Edge beds and cultivate soil lightly. Continue to weed flower and vegetable gardens. Water deeply. Mulch to 4"–6" during hottest days of summer. Add to and turn compost pile. Cut herbs, flowers for drying. Place orders for fall planting. Lawn care: raise mower during hottest weather; water weekly if needed.

Gulf & South Atlantic Coasts

Continue rose care program. Continue to cultivate lightly, weed, water deeply. Add to and turn compost pile. Continue to cut herbs and flowers for drying. Prepare new beds for fall planting. Place seed, bulb, plant orders for fall planting. Try new varieties. Lawn care: raise mower during hottest weather; water frequently.

Pacific Southwest & the Desert

Continue rose care program. Continue cutting herbs, flowers for drying. Pull, compost, and replace spent vegetables and annuals. Water deeply, especially newly planted material, avocado, and citrus. Place seed and plant orders for fall planting. Lawn care: raise mower during hottest weather; water frequently.

Pacific Northwest

Cultivate beds lightly to lessen compaction, weeds. Continue to pull and compost spent annuals, vegetable crops. Replant bare spots. Weed and water as necessary. Train plants growing on trellises, poles. Place orders for fall planting. Lawn care: raise mower during hottest weather—do not scalp lawn.

Rocky Mountains & the Plains

Protect newly set trees from sunscald with burlap or tree wrap. Stake floppy plants. Cultivate soil lightly. Edge and weed beds. Remulch if necessary. Cut herbs, flowers for drying. Pull and replace spent crops. Place fall planting orders. Lawn care: maintain at 3"; water as needed.

year _____

DESIGNING WITH ANNUALS

Use annuals freely in the garden and in containers for colorful seasonal effects. There are enough flower colors and forms, and foliage colors, textures, and shapes to provide an annual for every use. There are 3-inch alyssum and 6-foot Mexican sunflowers; there are moisture-loving forget-me-nots and drought-resistant African daisies, California poppies, and gypsophila. Pansies, sweet peas, and snapdragons thrive in cool temperatures, while marigolds, zinnias, and portulaca like hot temperatures. Most annuals prefer sun, but impatiens, begonias, and nicotiana do well in the shade.

Annuals will perform best if deadheaded regularly. Deadheading prevents the formation of seed and encourages rebloom. Most commercially grown annuals are hybrids and the seed they produce will probably revert to less desirable colors. For this reason it is best to pull and compost spent plants and start the next season with new seeds or seedlings. Annuals are shallow-rooted plants that with good drainage require only 4 to 6 inches of soil preparation. Most annuals are disease- and insect-resistant, so regular fertilizing with a water-soluble fertilizer and regular watering complete their care program.

Use annuals by themselves in beds and borders that are formal or informal, or in free-form island beds placed toward the edge of a major garden space. As in any planting design, the tall plants belong at the back (or in the center of island beds), medium-sized plants in the middle, and low-mounding or ground-cover plants in the foreground. Annuals encourage experimentation and give immediate results. If you like the results, you can reproduce them next year or improve upon the design; if you do not like the results, you can compost the plants and try something new.

The intense colors of many annuals can be overwhelming in a small-scale setting, so their use requires restraint. Masses of flaming yellow, orange, pink, and red can be an eyesore against a red brick wall. Use a limited, softer palette and fewer varieties of flowers; plant with gray-leaved foliage plants like dusty miller to blend colors and yield a more subtle look. Pastel and white gardens are especially effective at night. Include annual herbs—ornamental basil, borage, dill, fennel, oregano, variegated sage—in your scheme for flowers, foliage, and fragrance. If you are growing flowers for drying to use in bouquets, select a color scheme that complements the interior of your home.

Mix annuals into the existing framework of shrub and perennial borders to add summer and fall color. Their shallow roots will not intrude into permanent plantings, and they will fill the gaps left by faded, spring-flowering bulbs and perennials.

Sow annuals for quick, inexpensive color in newly dug areas waiting to be permanently planted, in bulb beds to hide unsightly foliage, with summer bulbs, or as fillers between young perennials that have not yet grown together.

Some annuals will languish and fade during warm, humid weather, but if deadheaded, sheared back, fertilized, and watered, will reassert themselves with cooler fall temperatures.

COOL-WEATHER ANNUALS: calendula, annual carnation, clarkia, cornflower, larkspur, nemesia, most pansies, primula, sweet pea.

WARM-WEATHER ANNUALS: ageratum, alyssum, browallia, celosia, four-o'clocks *(Mirabilis),* gaillardia, gazania, globe amaranth *(Gomphrena globosa),* marigold, nicotiana, salvia species, sunflower, tithonia, verbena, zinnia.

WHITE AND PASTEL ANNUALS: ageratum, alyssum, globe amaranth, China aster *(Callistephus chinensis),* wax begonia, bells of Ireland *(Molucella),* cleome, dianthus, heliotrope, larkspur, lobelia, nicotiana, nigella, petunia, salvia, snapdragon.

HOT COLORS: plumed celosia, coreopsis *(Coreopsis tinctoria),* cosmos *(Cosmos bipinnatus, C. sulphureus),* marigold, nasturtium, perilla, portulaca, red salvia *(Salvia coccinea),* sunflower *(helianthus* spp.), tithonia; for tropical foliage: castor bean *(Ricinus),* canna lily, coleus, rhubarb chard, 'Coppertone' hibiscus.

DRY AREAS: alyssum, cleome, euphorbia *(Euphorbia marginata),* gaillardia, helianthus, ice plant *(Mesembryanthemum crystallinum),* melampodium, mirabilis, morning glories, nasturtiums, phlox, poppies, portulaca, sanvitalia.

SEMISHADY AREAS: begonia, coleus, impatiens, fuchsia, monkey flower *(Mimulus),* nicotiana *(Nicotiana sylvestris),* torenia, vinca *(Catharanthus roseus).*

WILD GARDENS: dry areas: alyssum, bishop's flower *(Ammi majus),* coreopsis, cornflower, cosmos, gaillardia, godetias, larkspur, nicotiana spp., poppies; damp areas: forget-me-not, mignonette, primula.

WINDOW BOXES: ageratum, alyssum, African daisy *(Arctotis),* geranium *(Pelargonium),* fuchsia, ice plant, impatiens, lobelia, dwarf marigold, melampodium, nasturtium, pansies, cascading petunia, portulaca, Swan River daisy *(Brachycome),* verbena, vinca.

TALL ANNUALS (some can be grown as standards): cleome, lantana, marguerite, nicotiana, salvia, sunflowers *(Helianthus* spp.).

SHRUBBY ANNUALS: lavatera *(Lavatera trimestris),* kochia.

SPREADING ANNUALS: African daisy, ice plant, portulaca, garden verbena *(Verbena x hybrida),* vinca, creeping zinnia *(Sanvitalia).*

ANNUAL GRASSES: cloud grass *(Agrostis nebulosa),* quaking grass *(Brizia* spp.), annual fountain grass *(Pennisetum* spp.), Job's tears *(Coix lacryma-Jobi).*

ANNUAL VINES FOR VERTICAL FOLIAGE AND COLOR: canary vine *(Tropaeolum peregrinum),* cypress vine, hops *(Humulus),* hyacinth bean *(Dolichos lablab),* morning glory, moonflower *(Ipomoea Mexicana alba),* nasturtium, sweet pea, scarlet runner bean, thunbergia.

Any of the annuals just mentioned can be grown in containers. Sow annuals in pots to plunge into bare spots when flowering and remove when the bloom is over. Use them to fill a small space or to add temporary color close to the house. Or use them to fill window boxes or hanging baskets, or to add color to poolsides, decks, terraces, entrances, and courtyards. Be sure the mature size of the annual is neither too tall and leggy nor too small and insignificant for its container. Annuals are especially suited to containers because they are not permanent inhabitants of the garden but instead add exciting color and variety, if only for a season.

Annuals need to be replaced each year but are well worth the effort.

Buccolic vegetable garden.

Vegetables and Herbs

Today vegetable gardens are no longer relegated to a "sensible," often hidden plot, but are recognized as an addition to the landscape. A beautiful garden incorporates edible and ornamental herbs and vegetables into the mixed border or into containers on decks and terraces. In spring, yellow and orange marigolds edge the salad garden. Lettuces of various leaf colors and patterns contrast with chives that display their round, purple blossoms and act as an accent to late spring-blooming bulbs. Globe artichokes develop their dramatic, fountainlike form at the back of the border or in containers on the terrace. Their large edible buds turn into fragrant, lavender-blue thistles if not eaten, and these can be dried for flower arrangements.

During hot summer months when flowers wilt and gardens languish, peppers are ripening behind the dwarf zinnias and eye-catching eggplant and okra are just coming to maturity. Hyacinth vine is dangling its purple bean pods on the trellis, where it intertwines with morning glories. The stems of rhubarb chard are turning red. Bronze fennel waves its ferny foliage over gray-green, rough-leafed comfrey. As fall arrives, asparagus fronds turn golden at the back of the border or at the end of the vegetable garden. Lowbush blueberries, used as ground cover under azaleas and rhododendrons, turn deep red. Ornamental kale and cabbage can be eaten or left as a surreal presence in the winter snow.

If cooking with fresh herbs and growing and eating homegrown vegetables in quantity are your interest, however, then the most practical system is still an old-fashioned kitchen garden. Designing a kitchen garden that is utilitarian does not mean it cannot be attractive. One expects and is rewarded and pleased by order and neatness in a vegetable garden. To produce the largest quantity in the smallest space in the shortest time is the object. This requires planning and hard work, but you only have to visit George Washington's restored vegetable garden at Mount Vernon to see what a beautiful wall, spacious walks, a raised cistern, espaliered fruit trees, and a beehive can do.

Northeast
Late summer, heat and humidity

Mid-Atlantic
Late summer, heat and humidity

Mid-South
Late summer, heat and humidity

Gulf & South Atlantic Coasts
Late summer, heat and humidity

Pacific Southwest & the Desert
Hot, dry, summer conditions prevail

Pacific Northwest
Late summer heat

Rocky Mountains & the Plains
Hot, dry, summer conditions prevail

year _____

GARDENING GUIDE ~ PLANTING

Northeast
Plant, transplant broadleaf evergreens, especially hollies. Plant fall-blooming bulbs, madonna lilies, chrysanthemums for fall color. Start biennials in nursery bed or permanent position in garden. Divide and transplant spring- and early summer-blooming perennials. Sow cool-season vegetables.

Mid-Atlantic
Plant, transplant broadleaf evergreens, especially hollies. Plant fall-blooming bulbs, madonna lilies, chrysanthemums for fall color, pansy seedlings. Divide crowded spring- and early summer-blooming perennials, ground covers. Sow warm- and cool-season vegetables for fall crops. Transplant Brussels sprouts.

Mid-South
Plant fall-blooming bulbs, chrysanthemums for fall color. Divide and rejuvenate summer-blooming perennials. Start cool-season annuals in flats to transplant to garden in October. Sow warm- and cool-season vegetables. Transplant cabbage-family seedlings to garden. Begin to pot up herbs for indoor use.

Gulf & South Atlantic Coasts
Plant aquatic plants. Sow cool-season annuals, perennials, wildflowers in flats to set out in fall. Begin to sow cool-season vegetables and herbs. Begin to pot up herbs for a winter herb garden indoors. Continue to divide and plant crowded perennials, especially iris.

Pacific Southwest & the Desert
Start cool-season annuals and perennials in flats to set out in fall. Plant fall-flowering bulbs. Continue to divide perennials, especially iris. Continue to plant wildflower meadows. In warm areas, plant, transplant palms. *Zones 10, 9:* begin to sow cool-season vegetables and herbs, seed potatoes for fall planting in garden.

Pacific Northwest
Transplant cool-season annuals and biennials started last month. Plant fall-flowering bulbs. Continue to divide and plant overcrowded perennials. Sow cool-season vegetables for a fall crop.

Rocky Mountains & the Plains
Plant container-grown trees and shrubs, daylilies, peonies, poppies, iris, and fall-blooming bulbs. Start biennials in nursery bed or permanent position in garden. Dig and divide overcrowded spring- and early summer-blooming perennials. Sow cool-season vegetables for a fall crop.

PRUNING

Northeast

Prune water sprouts from dogwood, magnolias, fruit trees, wisteria for last time, trumpet vine after bloom. Lightly trim and shape overgrown hedges, foundation plantings, other woody plants. Trim and train espaliers and topiaries. Shear annuals lightly to promote fall bloom. Take herb cuttings.

Mid-Atlantic

Prune and train espaliers, topiaries, wisteria for last time. Lightly trim hedges. Lightly shear annuals to promote fall bloom. Take perennial and herb cuttings for propagation or to pot up for fresh use indoors.

Mid-South

Prune wisteria for last time. Train topiaries, espaliers. Check ties that may be strangling branches. Lightly shape hedges, foundation plantings, other woody plants. Prune berry bushes. Take softwood cuttings from trees, shrubs, perennials, house plants to increase plant stock.

Gulf & South Atlantic Coasts

Thin trees, shrubs as necessary, evergreens for last time. Do not trim spring-blooming plants. Train espaliers, topiaries. Check plant ties. Lightly cut back overgrown hedges, foundation plantings. Prune berries. Disbud camellias. Cut back, deadhead annuals, perennials. Pinch back chrysanthemums.

Pacific Southwest & the Desert

Thin and lightly shear trees, shrubs as necessary, except spring-bloomers to save bloom buds. Train espaliers, topiaries. Check ties that may be strangling branches. Cut back and deadhead annuals, perennials. Prune blackberry and dewberry bushes after fruiting.

Pacific Northwest

Train espaliers, topiaries. Check ties that may be strangling branches. Cut back and deadhead annuals, perennials, crape myrtle to prolong bloom. Disbud camellias if fewer, larger blossoms are desired. Lightly shear overgrown hedges, foundation plantings. Prune berry bushes that have finished producing.

Rocky Mountains & the Plains

Prune water sprouts from fruit trees. Lightly trim overgrown hedges, foundation plantings. Cut back and deadhead annuals, perennials to prolong bloom. Take perennial herb cuttings. Train espaliers, topiaries. Check ties that may be strangling branches.

FERTILIZING & GARDEN HIGHLIGHTS

year _____

Northeast

Continue to fertilize annuals, container plants, house plants monthly, chrysanthemums weekly. Fertilize vegetables, strawberry plants.

Highlights. Annuals; perennials; climbers: autumn clematis, hyacinth vine, rose; shrubs: blue spirea, hypericum, Peegee hydrangea; trees: ailanthus, sophora, sourwood.

Mid-Atlantic

Fertilize chrysanthemums weekly; annuals, container plants, house plants monthly; leafy vegetables.

Highlights. Annuals; perennials, including water lilies; flowering climbers; shrubs: althaea, blue spirea, butterfly bush, Peegee hydrangea, vitex; trees: sophora.

Mid-South

Fertilize annuals, chrysanthemums, container plants, house plants, vegetables.

Highlights. Summer-blooming bulbs, annuals, and perennials; shrubs: althaea, bottlebush, buckeye, butterfly bush, clethra, gardenia, hibiscus, hypericum; trees: crape myrtle.

Gulf & South Atlantic Coasts

Fertilize annuals, container plants, house plants, chrysanthemums, vegetable seedlings.

Highlights. Annual bulbs; perennials: datura, daylilies, hosta, ixora, liriope, ornamental grasses, phlox, plumbago, water lilies.

Pacific Southwest & the Desert

Fertilize annuals, container plants, house plants. Add iron chelates if necessary. Feed chrysanthemums. Fertilize vegetables, berries, strawberries.

Highlights. Annuals; perennials; flowering vines; shrubs: abelia, fuchsia, gardenia, jasmine, oleander; trees: eucalyptus, silk tree.

Pacific Northwest

Fertilize annuals, container plants, house plants summering outside, chrysanthemums until buds show color. Fertilize vegetable seedlings, strawberries.

Highlights. Annuals; perennials, including summer lilies; shrubs: butterfly bush, Peegee hydrangea, tamarisk.

Rocky Mountains & the Plains

Fertilize annuals, container plants, house plants summering outside, chrysanthemums, vegetable seedlings, strawberries. Spray fruit trees.

Highlights. Annual bulbs: canna, dahlia, gladiolus, montbretia; perennials; climbers; shrubs: althaea, caryopteris, hydrangea, potentilla, tamarisk.

GARDEN MAINTENANCE

Northeast

Continue to cut herbs, flowers to dry. Remove weeds before they go to seed. Pull and compost spent annuals and vegetables. Check house plants summering outside. Order spring-flowering bulbs. Lawn care: begin major lawn work—thatch deeply, top-dress, seed low areas and bare spots, seed or sod new lawn, mow when new grass is 3" high.

Mid-Atlantic

Aerate old lawns to promote root growth. Continue to cut herbs, flowers to dry. Continue to pull, compost spent annuals, crops. Weed, water. Clean out cold frame. Order spring-flowering bulbs, perennials for fall planting. Lawn care: begin major lawn work—test soil, adjust pH, thatch deeply, top-dress low spots, seed bare spots, water.

Mid-South

Remulch flower beds, shrub borders, vegetable garden. Remove weeds before they set seed. Continue to add to and turn compost pile. Do not compost grass clippings treated with herbicide. Place orders for fall planting. Lawn care: control lawn diseases, water deeply if season is dry, mow regularly.

Gulf & South Atlantic Coasts

Continue rose care. Clean up rose, flower, vegetable beds. Dispose of fallen leaves, deadwood. Remulch. Continue to weed, water. Check house plants summering outside. Order bulbs for fall planting. Lawn care: sow or sod Bermuda lawns, fertilize warm-season grasses, continue to mow and water regularly.

Pacific Southwest & the Desert

Continue rose care program: deadhead, spray, fertilize. Clean up fallen leaves. Water deeply. Stake tall perennials. Train plants growing on trellises and poles. Prepare beds for fall planting. Divide overcrowded gladiolus. Lawn care: fertilize warm-season grasses, continue to mow and water.

Pacific Northwest

Continue rose care program. Continue to cut herbs, flowers for drying. Clean up flower beds. Remulch trees, shrubs. Continue to irrigate deeply, especially azaleas, which are setting buds now. Check house plants summering outside. Lawn care: fertilize warm-season grasses, continue to mow and water deeply, watch for insects and diseases.

Rocky Mountains & the Plains

Continue to cut herbs, flowers to dry. Remove weeds before they set seed. In colder areas, gradually cut back on watering to harden off plants. Place orders for fall planting. Lawn care: begin major lawn work—test soil, adjust pH, thatch deeply; seed or sow a new lawn, keep well watered, cut new grass when 3" high.

DESIGNING WITH VEGETABLES AND HERBS

The ideal site for a basic, rectangular vegetable garden is a gently sloping, open, sunny, south-facing piece of ground, such as Thomas Jefferson's vegetable garden at Monticello. Vegetables and herbs have definite requirements that must be met if they are to be successfully grown. They need warm temperatures (above 60°), a minimum of six hours of sunlight a day, shelter from the wind, friable and well-drained soil, fertilizer, sufficient water, and protection from weeds, insects, and diseases.

Accommodations can be made if conditions are less than perfect. Planting in raised beds improves drainage and allows the soil to warm more rapidly in the spring. Hedges or fences reduce exposure problems. Removing nearby plants with greedy roots that extend into the garden eliminates competition, and limbing up nearby trees allows more light into the garden. A convenient water supply is necessary: an irrigation system, a nearby hose bib, or a cistern or barrel to hold sun-warmed water. Careful weeding and deep mulching control weeds; companion planting and crop rotation slow down insects and diseases.

Three important adjuncts to a well-managed garden are a cold frame to greatly lengthen the production season, a lath house to shade tender or cool-season plants from the sun, and a compost pile to recycle garden refuse and weeds into humus and mulch.

How you put all these elements together can be worked out to scale on graph paper. Think of the garden as a design element in the landscape, one that keeps its shape in winter as well as summer. Surround it with a fence or hedge to keep out intruders and to hold the design together. Add some choice evergreens in topiary form for sculptural interest and incorporate espaliered fruit trees and berry bushes to give it winter interest. Edge the beds with bricks or boards and mulch or pave the paths to ease maintenance and give a sense of order and purpose. Place a trellis for grapes or flowering vines in the background. Add a bench under it where the weary gardener can rest.

Within the garden area, there are some choices. You can plant in single rows, wide rows, or 4-foot blocks. Single rows require many paths but allow cultivating with power tools. Tomatoes and potatoes are easy to handle in single rows. Wide or double rows, as wide as 3 feet, are adaptable to salad greens, root crops, and herbs. Planting squares, or blocks that can be reached from all sides, lend themselves to many small crops. Place trellises and tall crops such as corn and pole beans to the north. Train vining plants—cucumbers, melons, squash, and tomatoes—on poles or trellises to save space, keep the vegetables clean, and provide some shade for tender salad greens in hot summer weather. Place perennial vegetables—asparagus, horseradish, rhubarb—and perennial herbs—chives, mints, tarragon—in areas where cultivating for new crops will not disturb their roots.

Add additional color and bloom to the classic vegetable garden with English daisies and calendulas, which bloom early in the spring. Include marigolds, garlic chives, nasturtiums, and hollyhocks. Make a hedge of lavender or gray santolina. Use parsley and chives for a long-

season edging, or alternate red- and green-leafed lettuce. Corn salad or land cress adds a neat finishing touch in late summer. Let a rambling rose spill over the fence. Grow scarlet runner beans or sweet peas over an arched gateway entrance.

Use edibles as ornamentals and decorate the entire garden. Incorporate vegetables and herbs into the classic flower border. Use amaranth, dark opal basil, red orach, and ornamental cabbage and kale for patches of bright color. Feature rhubarb as a focal point, and dill or bronze fennel as a feathery contrast to rough-leafed plants or ornamental grasses. For a tall accent, plant okra in place of hollyhocks in the back of the border or against a wall. The large showy blossoms, yellow or red and yellow, are followed by attractive green or red pods. Plant okra, pink zinnias, and ornamental peppers for late summer, when many perennials are through blooming. Plant asparagus with its ferny foliage at the back of the border, and at the end of the summer enjoy the red berries on the female plants. For strong vertical accents, plant Brussels sprouts and broccoli, letting them go to flower.

Grow vegetables and herbs that are not available commercially in your area, or that are unobtainable in good quality or in the varieties you prefer. There are seed companies that provide seeds for special crops, such as baby vegetables and unusual herbs for gourmets. Ask yourself what you are most interested in: herbs for drying, freezing, and potpourri? Or extra vegetables for canning, preserving, and freezing? Do you want only a salad and herb garden? Do you plan to have a berry patch and a small fruit orchard? Consider setting aside an area for cut flowers for the house or for drying; do not forget to leave space for planting rows of extra bulbs for early spring cutting.

Vegetables and herbs need not be grown only in large rectangles, rows, or squares isolated from other plants. If you lack a large space, look around for small areas that have sufficient sun and protection. Use dwarf, low-growing, and early-maturing varieties. Plant along the driveway, beside the kitchen door, in island beds carved out of sunny lawn areas, in window boxes, or in containers on the roof, balcony, or terrace.

Outline a container garden with dwarf fruit trees in planters. Arrange a trellis and train a flowering vine to climb up to provide summer color. Plant a large container in a sunny spot beside the kitchen door as a salad garden. Fill it with seedlings of Boston lettuce planted in a pattern, thyme to trail over the edge, Italian parsley, and garden chives. Center it with an ornamental kale or variegated mint. Add catmint for its gray foliage and blue blossoms. Or, in a small container, plant radishes, carrots, lettuce, and scallions, followed by spinach, a staked tomato, and a pepper plant. Use a long, deep window box for early peas, followed by bush beans or peppers and tomatoes. Plant asparagus in a deep box as a perennial crop. It will make a pretty background hedge.

Remember that container-grown plants need more consideration than those grown in the ground. Choose the largest planters possible because the soil in them dries rapidly. Terra-cotta pots allow more evaporation than fiberglass ones, and plants in them will need more water. Protection from the wind is important on roofs and balconies, but weeds there will not be a major problem. Special soil requirements can easily be met in planters. Eggplant, for example, difficult to grow in an ordinary garden because of soilborne diseases, grows well in fresh, sterilized soil. Choose a variety of container shapes and sizes that can be arranged for interest and to suit the vegetables and herbs you intend to plant in them. A strawberry jar can hold a handsome herb garden. Line a straw basket with a heavy plastic bag and plant lettuce in it. Use plastic walls designed to hold soil as vertical planting areas and as green space dividers. Use hanging baskets for growing herbs and dwarf vegetables. Plant in grow bags filled with soil mix if container weight is a problem; or to save money, fill heavy-duty garbage bags with soil and plant in them. Be sure to punch adequate holes for drainage. Disguise their sides with low pots of summer-blooming annuals. There are many interesting ways to incorporate vegetables into your garden.

A rich harvest of fruits and vegetables.

Soft mounds of ground cover make a wonderful carpet of textures and compatible colors.

GROUND COVERS FOR ALL SEASONS

Ground covers provide the horizontal plane in the landscape. Gardening with ground covers means planting a large number of the same kind of plant to grow together and cover the soil. Traditionally the choice was limited to low-growing periwinkle, pachysandra, and ivy. The extensive use of ground-cover plants originated as an American solution to landscape maintenance problems, and ground covers were once considered to be the practical workhorse plants of the landscape. Now they are featured to add visual interest, color, form, and texture to a garden, and they include a broader range of plants up to three or four feet tall.

The most versatile ground cover is grass. There is nothing more beautiful than a sweep of carefully manicured grass that visually sets off the house, flower border, or garden pool. Cut short and smooth and neatly edged, it is the best carpet of them all. It can be ruthlessly walked on and played on. For recreation it cannot be bettered.

But grass poses some problems. It is demanding of water, fertilizer, and mowing time. It offers no seasonal change of color, no flowers or berries. In some places it will not grow. In heavy shade, under beeches and maples, in competition with tree roots, or on dry, compacted or overly moist soils, it languishes. On steep banks and rocky slopes it is impossible to maintain.

There are alternatives—groups of plants that are ideal ground covers for areas that are shady, steep, rocky, moist, dry, or too exposed to the elements. Set close together, each plant helps its neighbor grow, and together they form a thick, protective ground cover of vegetation that blocks out the light, prevents the growth of weeds, and absorbs leaf fall from taller plants. With the assistance of various insects, fungi, and earthworms, the ground cover decomposes the litter and nourishes the soil and the plants growing in it. It is a permanent mulch. It reduces soil compaction, helps to conserve moisture, and keeps the roots of taller plants cool.

Ground covers can be evergreen—broadleaf or needle—or deciduous, and from 3 inches to 3 feet tall.

Northeast
Early frost is possible

Mid-Atlantic
Extreme heat still possible

Mid-South
Extreme heat still possible

Gulf & South Atlantic Coasts
Extreme heat still possible

Pacific Southwest & the Desert
Extreme heat and dry conditions prevail

Pacific Northwest
Varying weather patterns prevail

Rocky Mountains & the Plains
Early frost is possible

GARDENING GUIDE ~ PLANTING

Northeast

Plant, transplant broadleaf and needle evergreen trees and shrubs, ground covers, meadows, new perennials. Divide established clumps. Plant container-grown asters, chrysanthemums. Pot up herbs for indoor use, tender perennials to winter over in cold frame. Begin planting spring-flowering bulbs. Sow cool-season greens.

Mid-Atlantic

Plant, transplant evergreen trees and shrubs, ground covers, new perennials. Plant container-grown asters and chrysanthemums, daylilies, peonies, ornamental grasses, wildflower meadows. Divide and rejuvenate overgrown perennials. Pot up herbs for indoor use. Plant early spring-flowering bulbs. Sow cool-season vegetables.

Mid-South

Plant, transplant evergreen trees, shrubs, ground covers, and deciduous trees and shrubs after leaf fall. Plant new perennials, ornamental grasses. Divide established clumps. Sow wildflower meadows, cool-season annuals and vegetables. Set out cool-season annuals and vegetable seedlings.

Gulf & South Atlantic Coasts

Begin planting container-grown and mail-order plants. Divide ground covers. Transplant winter-blooming annuals to garden. Sow sweet peas. Continue planting wildflower meadows. Begin planting, transplanting spring- and summer-blooming perennials, summer-flowering true lilies. Sow cool-season vegetables and herbs.

Pacific Southwest & the Desert

Begin fall planting as temperatures cool. Divide ground covers. Transplant warm-season annuals for fall color. Begin setting out cool-season annuals. Sow sweet peas. Divide and rejuvenate perennials, especially iris. Begin planting South African and fall-flowering bulbs. Start cool-season annuals and perennials in flats.

Pacific Northwest

Begin planting, transplanting evergreen trees and shrubs. Divide ground covers. Replace straggly annuals with container-grown asters and chrysanthemums. Transplant cool-season annuals to garden. Sow cool-season vegetables, wildflower meadows. Divide and rejuvenate perennials. Begin planting true lilies.

Rocky Mountains & the Plains

Plant container-grown trees and shrubs. Plant, transplant deciduous trees and shrubs, ground covers. Plant new perennials, container-grown asters and chrysanthemums for fall color, early spring-blooming bulbs. Divide crowded perennials. Pot up herbs for indoor use, tender perennials to winter over in cold frame.

year _____

PRUNING

Northeast

Root-prune plants to ready them for spring transplanting, wisteria reluctant to bloom. Prune transplanted plants to compensate for root loss. Take perennial cuttings to root and winter over in cold frame, annual cuttings to root and use as flowering house plants.

Mid-Atlantic

Lightly trim shaggy hedges. Root-prune plants to prepare for spring transplanting, wisteria reluctant to bloom. Take perennial cuttings to root and winter over in cold frame, annual cuttings to root and use as flowering house plants.

Mid-South

Prune transplanted plants to compensate for root loss. Root-prune wisteria reluctant to bloom, plants to ready them for transplanting in the spring, especially broadleaf evergreens. Prune house plants before moving indoors.

Gulf & South Atlantic Coasts

Prune dead, diseased, weak branches of trees and large shrubs to protect from hurricane damage. Root-prune large plants to ready them for spring transplanting. Thin camellia buds if fewer, larger blooms are desired. Take hard- and softwood cuttings to increase plant stock.

Pacific Southwest & the Desert

Prune deadwood, weak and diseased branches of trees and large shrubs. Thin camellia buds to encourage larger blooms. Cut back and deadhead annuals, perennials to prolong bloom. Take hard- and softwood cuttings to increase plant stock.

Pacific Northwest

Prune deadwood, weak and diseased branches from trees and shrubs. Root-prune to ready large plants for spring transplanting. Thin camellia buds if fewer, larger blooms are desired. Deadhead annuals. Take hard- and softwood cuttings to increase plant stock.

Rocky Mountains & the Plains

Prune deadwood, weak and diseased branches from trees and shrubs. Lightly shear hedges. Prune newly transplanted trees and shrubs to compensate for root loss. Root-prune wisteria reluctant to bloom, large plants to ready them for spring transplanting. Take annual cuttings to use as flowering plants indoors.

FERTILIZING & GARDEN HIGHLIGHTS

Northeast

Fertilize annuals, container plants, house plants monthly. Feed peonies.

Highlights. Bulbs: autumn crocus, colchicum, hardy cyclamen, dahlia; perennials; climbers: autumn clematis, fleece vine, gold-flame honeysuckle; shrubs: althaea, butterfly bush, heather, rose.

Mid-Atlantic

Fertilize annuals, container plants, house plants monthly, peonies, wisteria.

Highlights. Bulbs; perennials: hardy ageratum, hardy begonia, ornamental grasses, perovskia; climbers: clematis; shrubs: caryopteris, heather, osmanthus, rose; trees: franklinia, larch.

Mid-South

Fertilize trees, shrubs, vines, ground covers to promote root growth, annuals, container plants.

Highlights. Bulbs; annuals; perennials: aster, chrysanthemum, Japanese anemone, ornamental grasses, sedum; shrubs: camellia, elaeagnus; trees: crape myrtle, fall-blooming cherry, franklinia.

Gulf & South Atlantic Coasts

Fertilize annuals, chrysanthemums, trees, shrubs, ground covers, perennials, vines, tropicals.

Highlights. Bulbs: canna, lycoris; annuals; perennials; shrubs: althaea, hibiscus, oleander, rose; trees: crape myrtle, coral tree, floss silk, Hong Kong orchid tree.

Pacific Southwest & the Desert

Fertilize established permanent plantings. Apply pre-emergent herbicide to dry landscapes.

Highlights. Bulbs: lycoris, nerine, sternbergia; annuals; perennials; climbers: clematis, guinea gold; shrubs: bottlebush, fuchsia, lantana, oleander, rose; trees: crape myrtle, eucalyptus, Hong Kong orchid tree, silk tree.

Pacific Northwest

Fertilize trees, shrubs, ground covers, vines to promote root bud growth, annuals, container plants.

Highlights. Autumn bulbs: crocus, dahlia, tritoma; annuals: begonia, celosia, impatiens, marigold, petunia, salvia; perennials; shrubs: elaeagnus, heather, Peegee hydrangea, rose.

Rocky Mountains & the Plains

Fertilize annuals, container plants, house plants monthly, and peonies with bonemeal.

Highlights. Bulbs; late annuals; perennials: aster, chrysanthemum, delphinium, ornamental grasses, sedum; shrubs: butterfly bush, caryopteris, rose.

year _____

GARDEN MAINTENANCE

year _____

Northeast

Begin fall cleanup. Prepare beds for fall and spring planting. Edge beds and mulch for weed and moisture control. Continue watering trees, shrubs until ground freezes. Protect plants from early frost. Begin moving house plants indoors. Continue rose care program. Lawn care: complete major work, apply broadleaf weed control.

Mid-Atlantic

Begin fall cleanup. Prepare beds for fall and spring planting. Edge existing beds and mulch for weed and moisture control. Water trees and shrubs until ground freezes. Begin moving house plants indoors. Tend roses. Allow amaryllis to dry out. Lawn care: complete major lawn work, keep new grass damp, mow when 3" high.

Mid-South

Begin fall cleanup. Pull spent annuals and vegetables, weed, edge beds, mulch. Continue watering. Prepare beds for fall and spring planting. Install a cold frame. Continue rose care. Lawn care: sow a new lawn, rework an established one; fertilize warm-season grasses; sow annual rye for winter color.

Gulf & South Atlantic Coasts

Prepare beds for fall and spring plantings. Continue layering or taking cuttings to increase stock. Prepare cold frames. Continue rose care. Lawn care: install new lawns or renovate establish ones; thatch, mow closely; seed or sod; keep moist.

Pacific Southwest & the Desert

Begin fall cleanup. Weed and cultivate. Water regularly, especially azaleas, camellias that are setting buds. Prepare beds for fall and spring plantings. Continue rose care. Lawn care: begin major work—seed or sod new lawns and renovate existing ones; spray for weeds; apply pre-emergent herbicide to Bermuda grass.

Pacific Northwest

Begin fall cleanup. Prepare cold frames, greenhouses. Service watering systems. Dispose of fallen fruit, spent vegetable crops. Lawn care: begin major lawn work—seed or sod new lawns, renovate established ones; aerate, level, seed, fertilize, keep moist; overseed warm-season grasses with annual rye.

Rocky Mountains & the Plains

Apply broadleaf weed control. Begin fall cleanup. Edge, weed, mulch beds, prepare for fall and spring plantings. Protect tender plants from frost. Lawn care: complete major work; keep new grass seed damp, mow when 3" high; feed established lawns. *Zones 5, 4:* after deciduous plants harden off, soak ground; move house plants indoors.

DESIGNING WITH GROUND COVERS

As a design element, ground covers link, accent, and define horizontal spaces. They offer a diversity of height, texture, and color while creating harmony in the landscape. They sweep over the ground, accenting the more important plantings, integrating and unifying disparate elements, and pulling the landscape together. Planted adjacent to lawns, they give them shape by breaking up the monotony of too much grass and outlining the shape of beds and plantings; bold drifts of liriope or mondo grass, for example, smooth out any suggestion of spottiness and make a pleasing transition between the shrub border and the grass. Ground covers can emphasize a garden design or pattern by leading the eye through the space.

Ground covers are like carpets. They are the horizontal plane in the landscape. The extensive use of ground-cover plants originated as an American solution to landscape maintenance problems. Traditionally the choice was limited to practical workhorse plants like periwinkle (*Vinca minor*), pachysandra, and ivy. Today, gardening with ground covers means planting any of a large number of the same kind of plant to grow together and cover the soil. This definition includes a broad range of plants up to 3 or 4 feet high that provide a variety of textures and colors while cutting down on maintenance, checking erosion, and reducing moisture loss.

Gray leaves and purple flowers is a tried-and-true color combination.

Ground-cover plants are usually thought of as flat-growing, but they have many different growing habits.

- ❦ Flat-growing or carpeting ground covers expand by runners that layer or put out new roots along their stems as they come in contact with the soil: creeping junipers, cotoneaster, periwinkle, ivy, lamiastrum, bearberry, some roses, and waldsteinia.

- ❦ Some ground covers form mounds that give a billowy effect if they are planted closely together: heathers and heaths, barberries, stephanandra, euonymus, and some junipers ('Bluechip', 'Tamariscifolia').

- ❦ Some ground covers are spreaders that increase by underground roots or shoots: ajuga, pachysandra, hypericum, sarcococca, and red-twig dogwood.

- ❦ Some perennials are clump-formers that grow from a central rootstock and make excellent ground covers: brunnera, gazania, hosta, bergenia, alchemilla, and many ornamental grasses.

- ❦ Some ground covers are sprawlers that have both erect and floppy stems: euonymus, cotoneaster, and some roses.

Ground covers can be mixed or planted with other kinds of plants; however, the plants must have the same cultural requirements.

In dense shade among competing tree roots, ivy, pachysandra, and lily of the valley are traditional alternatives to grass. They conceal exposed tree roots and reduce maintenance, especially around the base of large trees growing in the lawn or in areas where tree roots protrude into adjacent grass. Other shallow-rooted plants—epimedium, ajuga, dwarf hosta, lamiastrum, liriope, waldsteinia—can also be established in areas that are frequently dry and difficult to mow.

On shady woodland floors, if the hardiness zone permits, periwinkle and winter creeper (*Euonymus coloratus*) form evergreen carpets, while Canadian wild ginger, foam flower, star jasmine, sweet woodruff, hardy geraniums, strawberry begonia *(Saxifraga sarmentosa)*, tiarella, yellowroot, and creeping *Astilbe chinensis pumila* offer seasonal change.

In mass plantings, in open woodlands, low shrubs—Oregon grapeholly, leucothoe, paxistima, sarcococca, lowbush blueberry in acid soil, low azaleas—unify and anchor trees to the ground. Ferns and variegated forms of liriope and hosta brighten dark corners.

Terraced sunny slopes can be planted with low junipers, heather, cotoneasters, daylilies, helianthemum, winter-blooming jasmine, lavender, periwinkle, santolina, and sweet fern. Interplant with bulbs, perennials, ornamental grasses, and cascading, flowering shrubs like spirea to create handsome display areas.

Blanket uneven, steep, and rocky slopes and control erosion with euonymus, honeysuckle, Virginia creeper, junipers, cotoneaster, ground-cover roses, ice plant, weeping forsythia, ground bamboo, stephanandra; in the shade allow ivy and climbing hydrangea to sprawl.

Plant ground covers as barriers to help direct traffic and keep neighboring dogs from trespassing. Prickly juniper, barberry, low roses, red-berried coralberry, and moisture-loving yellowroot make neat, compact plantings.

Use a ground cover as a setting for bulbs. A low-growing, thick ground cover will not smother newly planted spring-blooming bulbs or keep the sun from their leaves as they ripen. Crocus will emerge from periwinkle or ajuga, daffodils from ivy, and lycoris from gray-leafed heather.

In plantings of slow-growing ground covers, add annuals the first year to fill in any gaps and cut down weeds before they are crowded out when the major plants converge.

Mix ground covers in a planting: mounding junipers with spreading junipers, junipers with cotoneaster, lamb's ears with santolina, lilyturf with dwarf azaleas, sedum with mugo pine.

Ground covers can solve many maintenance problems and lend themselves to endless creative uses.

NATURAL GARDENS

A natural garden emphasizes natural beauty, native plants, low maintenance, and lower water consumption. It may be the recreation of a wild garden, or a wilderness area that has been modified to highlight its inherent charm. Its great appeal lies in the fact that you are restoring and working with nature, rather than against it. By focusing on native plant materials and those that have adapted over time to a particular area, a natural gardener achieves a landscape that is ecologically sound and aesthetically appealing with minimum maintenance, cost, and time. By basing plant selections on their suitability to a particular site, the gardener can decide just how naturalistic or how self-sustaining the landscape will be. Meadow, prairie, and chaparral gardens, wetland and woodland gardens feature an abundance of indigenous plant material that offers habitats and a food supply to various birds, butterflies, insects, and small and large mammals.

Developing a "sense of place" is especially appropriate in a natural garden. Ecological conditions on the site, the terrain, the soil, and the climate, although they can be modified in part, should suggest the design and the choice of plants. A rocky outcropping covered with lichens and ferns dictates one sort of garden, a windswept beachfront covered with grasses and bayberry another, and a desert property of dunes and cactus yet another. The presence of a natural water source suggests a water garden, an informal pool, a bog, a stream, or a pond. An interest in the conservation of wildlife, and a desire for low maintenance will encourage the use of native plants.

One of the basic limitations set by our current environment is the amount of water available. The term *xeriscaping* is used to signify an approach to gardening based on limited water supplies. Xeriscaping focuses on planning and maintenance methods that reduce water consumption. Another factor is the need to recycle garden wastes as most public landfills will no longer accept lawn clippings or other garden refuse.

Still another is the contamination of the environment by the overuse of chemical fertilizers, pesticides, and herbicides to support unsuitable gardening practices such as large lawn areas. Concentrating on good planning and design, practical turf areas, appropriate plant selection, efficient irrigation, the recycling of garden wastes as compost and mulch, and limiting use of chemicals, fertilizers, and pest controls point the way to a more natural style of gardening.

Four environments around which a natural garden can be developed are desert, water, woodland, and meadow.

Northeast
Frost is possible

Mid-Atlantic
Early frost is possible

Mid-South
Early frost is possible

Gulf & South Atlantic Coasts
Random weather patterns prevail

Pacific Southwest & the Desert
Early frost is possible

Pacific Northwest
Early frost is possible

Rocky Mountains & the Plains
Frost is possible

GARDENING GUIDE ~ PLANTING

Northeast

Plant, transplant needle evergreen trees and shrubs, deciduous trees and shrubs after leaf fall. Continue planting early spring bulbs. Begin planting tulips. Divide perennials. Lift and store tender bulbs. Pot up hardy spring-blooming bulbs for forcing. *Zones 5, 4:* plant asparagus, berry bushes.

Mid-Atlantic

Plant, transplant evergreen trees and shrubs, deciduous trees and shrubs after leaf fall, berry bushes, asparagus. Continue dividing perennials, planting spring bulbs. Begin planting tulips. Sow spinach to winter over. Pot up hardy spring-blooming bulbs for forcing.

Mid-South

Plant, transplant evergreen and deciduous trees and shrubs, ground covers, roses, asparagus, rhubarb, berry bushes. Divide late perennials. Plant early spring-blooming bulbs. Set out biennial seedlings. Sow or set out cool-season annuals. Sow cool-season vegetables in cold frame. Pot up hardy spring-blooming bulbs for forcing.

Gulf & South Atlantic Coasts

Begin planting, transplanting evergreen trees and shrubs, ground covers, vines, roses, lilies, pansies, asparagus, berries, rhubarb, Jerusalem artichokes. Divide perennials, ornamental grasses. Begin planting early spring-blooming bulbs. Sow cool-season annuals and winter vegetables and herbs in cold frame.

Pacific Southwest & the Desert

Begin planting evergreen trees and shrubs, ground covers, vines, fruit trees, berry bushes, rhubarb, figs, grapes. Continue dividing and planting perennials. Plant lilies. Set out cool-season annuals. Begin planting spring-blooming bulbs. Sow cool-season vegetables. Pot up hardy bulbs for forcing, herbs for indoors.

Pacific Northwest

Begin planting deciduous trees and shrubs, ground covers, vines, ornamental grasses, fruit trees, berries, asparagus, rhubarb. Continue dividing, planting, transplanting perennials, lilies. Begin planting spring-blooming bulbs. Dig and store tender bulbs. Sow cool-season vegetables and herbs in cold frame.

Rocky Mountains & the Plains

Plant, transplant container-grown and deciduous trees and shrubs after leaf fall, asparagus, rhubarb, berry bushes. Continue planting spring-blooming bulbs. Begin planting tulips. Continue dividing perennials. Pot up hardy spring-blooming bulbs for forcing.

PRUNING

Northeast

Prune late summer-blooming shrubs (abelia, althaea, butterfly bush, clethra, hydrangea, hypericum) when fully dormant. Prune and fasten climbers against wind damage. Take hardwood cuttings to increase plant stock.

Mid-Atlantic

Prune and fasten climbers against wind damage. Take hardwood cuttings to increase plant stock.

Mid-South

Prune and fasten climbers against wind damage. Take hardwood cuttings to increase plant stock.

Gulf & South Atlantic Coasts

Continue fall pruning of weak, dead, diseased wood. Prune and fasten climbers against wind damage. Root-prune wisteria reluctant to bloom. Take hardwood cuttings to increase plant stock.

Pacific Southwest & the Desert

Prune trees, shrubs, vines, roses as they finish blooming to remove deadwood only. Prune climbers against wind damage. Root-prune wisteria reluctant to bloom. Take hardwood cuttings.

Pacific Northwest

Prune trees, shrubs, vines, roses to remove deadwood only. Prune and fasten climbers against wind damage. Root-prune wisteria reluctant to bloom.

Rocky Mountains & the Plains

Prune late summer-blooming shrubs (abelia, althaea, butterfly bush, clethra, hydrangea, hypericum) when fully dormant. Prune and fasten climbers against wind damage. Take hardwood cuttings.

year _____

Fertilizing & Garden Highlights

Northeast

Fertilize deciduous and broadleaf and needle evergreen trees and shrubs when dormant.

Highlights. Perennials: aconitum, aster, boltonia, chrysanthemum, ornamental grasses, sedum, wildflowers; fall color: berries of chokeberry, cotoneaster, mountain ash, pyracantha, viburnum; changing foliage of shrubs, vines, trees.

Mid-Atlantic

Fertilize deciduous and needle evergreen trees and shrubs when dormant.

Highlights. Late annuals; shrubs: elaeagnus, osmanthus, sasanqua camellia; fall color: berries, fruits, changing fall foliage.

Mid-South

Fertilize trees and shrubs when dormant. Check azalea pH and correct if necessary. Apply brown patch fungicide.

Highlights. Fall bulbs, annuals, and perennials; shrubs: camellia, osmanthus, rose; fall color: berries, fruits; changing fall foliage of shrubs, vines, trees.

Gulf & South Atlantic Coasts

Fertilize trees and shrubs when dormant to stimulate root growth. Feed annuals, container plants, house plants.

Highlights. Late annuals and perennials; fall color: berries of aucuba, holly, nandina, pyracantha, viburnum; foliage of Bradford pear, Chinese pistachio, crape myrtle, ginkgo, maple, sweet gum.

Pacific Southwest & the Desert

Fertilize trees, shrubs, established bulb beds, established and newly planted annuals, container plants, house plants, winter vegetables.

Highlights. Late annuals, perennials, and vines; shrubs: abelia, barberry, cassia, hibiscus, osmanthus, plumbago, rose.

Pacific Northwest

Fertilize deciduous and evergreen trees, shrubs. Feed established bulb beds, container plants, house plants.

Highlights. Fall bulbs: crocus; late annuals; perennials: aster, chrysanthemum, ornamental grasses, sedum, tritoma; shrubs: heather, rose; trees: fall-blooming cherry, dogwood.

Rocky Mountains & the Plains

Fertilize deciduous and broadleaf and needle evergreen trees and shrubs when dormant.

Highlights. Fall color: berries of autumn olive, barberry, buckthorn, chokeberry, cotoneaster, dogwood, hawthorn, holly, mountain ash, pyracantha, snowberry, viburnum; changing foliage.

year _____

GARDEN MAINTENANCE

Northeast

Water broadleaf evergreens, newly planted trees and shrubs, bulb beds thoroughly before ground freezes. Continue fall cleanup. Prepare roses for winter. Place tender plants in cold frame. Clean up perennial, annual, vegetable beds. Prepare for spring planting. Begin feeding birds mixed seed and suet. Lawn care: continue mowing and watering new grass.

Mid-Atlantic

Continue fall cleanup. Lift and store tender bulbs. Weed, shape, edge beds. Pull and compost spent plants. Protect tender vegetable crops if frost threatens. Move remaining house plants indoors. Begin feeding birds mixed seed and suet. Feed fish in lily ponds until water freezes. Lawn care: continue mowing and watering new grass.

Mid-South

Rake and compost leaves regularly. Pull spent crops. Weed, edge, mulch beds. Slow down on watering to prepare plants for cooler weather. Move warm-season plants to cold frame. Dig and store summer-blooming bulbs. Water new bulb beds. Lawn care: continue mowing and watering new grass.

Gulf & South Atlantic Coasts

Begin fall cleanup. Rake regularly. Remove spent plants. Weed, edge, mulch beds. Prepare new beds. Dig and store tender summer-blooming bulbs. As weather cools, slow down on watering. Move foliage plants indoors. Lawn care: overseed warm-season grasses with annual rye, keep moist; keep grass at 2" going into winter.

Pacific Southwest & the Desert

Continue rose care, fall cleanup. Dispose of diseased plant material. Prepare beds for fall and spring plantings. Lift and store tender bulbs. Install a cold frame. Lawn care: sow annual winter rye, cool-season grasses; fertilize; *zone 10*—apply weed-and-feed combination to warm-season grasses.

Pacific Northwest

Clean up perennial, annual beds. Weed, shape, edge beds. Dispose of diseased plant material. Cut perennial stalks to 4"–5". Lift and store tender bulbs. Water newly planted trees and shrubs, bulb beds. Protect late vegetables. Lawn care: continue to seed cool-season lawns, feed cool-season grasses.

Rocky Mountains & the Plains

Continue fall cleanup. Clean up perennial, annual, vegetable beds. Prepare roses for winter. Lift and store tender bulbs. Pot up hardy bulbs for forcing. Water newly planted broadleaf and shallow-rooted trees and shrubs, bulb beds. Begin feeding birds mixed seed and suet. Lawn care: continue mowing and watering new grass.

DESIGNING A NATURAL GARDEN

DESERT GARDEN

Many gardeners in the Rocky Mountains and Southwest face a harsh environment of alkaline or saline soil, high elevations (with widely contrasting day- and nighttime temperatures), hot sun, desiccating winds, and lack of moisture. An appropriate solution is the development of an oasis garden that makes full use of any existing moisture. Windbreaks help. Use the house as a wind deflector. Plant drought-resistant, native ground covers, shrubs, and trees at the perimeter of the property to filter dust, moderate temperatures, and create privacy.

Pave outdoor living spaces adjacent to the house to reduce the area requiring irrigation. Include a small lush carpet of warm-season grass. Make these areas inviting by shading them with deciduous trees or vine canopies that contribute summertime shade and allow warming sunlight in winter. For a lush look, add groupings of containers filled with foliage and flowering plants. Use Arizona sycamore, desert willow, desert olive, oaks, acacia, Russian olive, and tamarisk to provide a framework for the patio and interesting winter silhouettes and shadow patterns. Insulate a northwest-facing wall in summer or make windbreaks with pine species, Arizona cypress, and junipers.

On a hilly site, build retaining walls or regrade to terrace steep slopes. These measures will decrease erosion problems and control and channel water runoff to planted areas, reducing the need for supplemental watering. By altering the natural grade of a broad expanse of ground, a flat site can be made more interesting and water more efficiently used. Even slight changes of elevation create unique microclimates. Low spots will accommodate thirstier plants and high spots the more self-sufficient ones. Planting beds can be as much as 4 inches lower than the soil level in lawn areas. Soil in planting beds close to the house can be improved with compost to retain moisture.

Select and group plants according to their moisture requirements. Restrict the most moisture-loving plants to the area close to the house, patio, and hose bib for easier maintenance. Use mass plantings of less thirsty, more adaptable plants next, and rugged, self-sufficient ones at the property edge. These boundary plants will help blend your property with the surrounding landscape.

This environmentally sensitive design will allow you to use a broad palette of seasonally flowering shrubs and perennials, reduce water use, and provide a varied and interesting landscape. Plant choice will vary according to local elevation and temperature range. Tempting as it is to plant large specimens collected from the wild, you will find that they do not establish well because they expend their energy on developing a new root system instead of growing above the ground. Choose smaller, local, nursery-grown stock that will adapt rapidly.

DAMP GARDEN

Designing a damp, or wet, garden brings a whole new range of plant material. Existing damp or wet spots should be encouraged to provide homes for bog or marsh plants that can be maintained in hot, dry, summer months with hidden irrigation systems. Or, excavate an informal pool. It will look its best at the lowest point in the garden. Use the excavated earth to shape a pleasing setting for the pool. Keep it filled to the brim, with all signs of artificial materials hidden from view, and surround it with moisture-loving plants. Add moving water in an artificial stream to flow naturally down an incline or spill into the pool. Design the pool and stream using reinforced concrete, a rubberized liner, or preformed plastic pool shapes. Use a pump to recycle water through the stream or through a jet. A shallow pool will attract birds; a deep pool will draw frogs, turtles, ducks, and raccoons.

A pool featuring plants needs at least six hours of sun per day. Place the pool so that major trees and shrubs are to the north, the pool is not shaded out, and it is far enough away to keep out most vegetative litter. Keep at least two-thirds of a pool's surface clear of plants to avoid a choked or overgrown look and to reflect the sky. Keep a section of the margin of the pool clear, or plant with low-growing plants to provide a good view of the water upon approaching it. Hide the rest of the rim with groupings of large-leafed plants, such as rodgersia or *Rheum palmatum,* contrasted with bold, vertical spikes of water iris or plumes of goatsbeard *(Aruncus dioicus)* and water rue *(Thalictrum aquilegifolium)*. Exclude plants not generally found near water or bright-colored plants that would distracted from the sense of tranquillity.

WOODLAND GARDEN

In preparing a site for a woodland garden, clean out underbrush, weak saplings, and fallen debris. Thin out canopy trees to allow more sunlight to reach the ground. Limb up major trees and clean up their trunks to raise the tree canopy and enhance the natural form of the trees, transforming them into columns rising above the woodland floor. Next, develop spaces within the woods. Lay out paths and direct views. Plant understory trees, shrubs, and perennials to expand the blooming sequence. Include winter-flowering shrubs, winter hazel *(Corylopsis* spp.), wintersweet *(Chimonanthus praecox),* and witch hazel *(Hamamelis* spp.). Create small sitting areas by carefully grouping shrubs. Place a fallen log for a resting spot. Incorporate a small informal pool to enhance the habitat for wildlife. Include evergreens (acid-loving hollies, rhododendrons, azaleas, laurel, pieris, and leucothoe, as well as hemlock, spruce, and other needle evergreens) for winter interest, to obstruct undesirable views, and as a background for deciduous shrubs and trees.

Screening will make an open, flat wood more interesting and provide shelter for tender plants. By carefully ordering the underplanting, you can focus attention within the woodland, forming glades to provide sheltered planting areas for wildflowers—primroses, violets, celandine poppies, phlox, trillium, jack-in-the-pulpit, wood anemones, and bulbs, followed by shade-loving ferns, hostas, and martagon lilies. Even ground-cover plants such as winter creeper, periwinkle, and ivy will clothe the forest floor, making a green background for sweeps of bulbs in the spring before trees leaf out.

A woodland can also be started from scratch on a corner of your property to reduce a bare, broad span of lawn. If you stop mowing to the edge of your property, native growth will soon reappear, and you can obtain a seminatural look by planting saplings or ornamental trees that might grow in adjacent woods and letting them develop slowly. Japanese maples, shadbush *(Amelanchier* spp.), redbud *(Cercis* spp.), dogwood *(Cornus* spp.), sassafras *(S. albidum),* and silk tree *(Albizia julibrissin)* all thrive at the woodland edge and help blend the woodland garden into formal areas.

MEADOW GARDEN

A meadow may be an abandoned field or one that has been grazed over for many years and remained open rather than reverting to woodland. A natural meadow contains a mix of grasses and wildflowers. Man-made wildflower meadows can be established where appropriate. They fit naturally along the edge of ponds or woodlands. They are an alternative to extensive lawn areas. In a small garden, a "meadow" might even be as simple as a corner devoted to native plants or the area under a clump of trees that you no longer wish to mow. Many flowering plants that emerge under these conditions are highly ornamental.

Unlike a formal, evenly textured lawn, which is visually static, a meadow is informal and diverse. It offers an interplay of varied annual and perennial plants that are attractive to bees, butterflies, birds, and small mammals. An occasional tree or shrub is not out of place, but woody plants should be kept to a minimum. Most flower meadows require at least 15–25 inches of rainfall each year or deep supplemental watering. Exposure, soil type, and temperatures determine which seeds will grow and when they will germinate. Wildflower seeds are variable to ensure their survival in a harsh environment; many need periods of extreme cold, heat, or even fire to germinate. The composition of the seed mix is critical and needs to be specified for your area. A proper mix consists of 25 percent noninvasive grasses, 30 percent annual and biennial seeds for first-year coverage, and 45 percent perennial seeds that will take over the meadow the second year and become its mainstay. Native bulbs can be added to meadows: allium, brodiaea, camassia, fritillaria, and various lilies.

Preparing a site for a meadow requires persistence. Do not strip the site. It is essential to rid the area of competition from undesirable weeds and invasive woody plants, but not at the expensive of creating erosion problems. Work around and preserve any existing attractive

vegetation. Till and water the rest of the soil to encourage germination of all undesirable annual weed seeds so they can be identified and sprayed with a systemic herbicide. Repeat the process as many times as necessary to eliminate seedlings that appear, and until a satisfactory weed-free seedbed is created.

Till 6 to 8 inches deep any areas to be planted with seeds and 12 inches deep any areas planned for massing of perennial seedlings such as daylilies, black-eyed Susans, butterfly weed, sedums, ornamental grasses, and naturalizing bulbs.

Plant wildflower meadows in the spring or fall to take advantage of natural rainfall. Weed the meadow late in its first summer by snipping off the blossoms of any undesirable plants before they go to seed instead of pulling them, which disturbs the ground and encourages remaining dormant weed seeds. Mow the meadow in late fall after a hard freeze when seedpods have formed and seeds have scattered. Or you can leave desirable ornamental pods and grasses as decorative elements through the winter and mow in early spring.

Meadows can be given a neat appearance (important in suburban areas) by bordering them with a wide mowing strip or drifts of native shrubs. The edge of the driveway or a walkway also serves to define an edge. Mowing a simple curving path through the grasses will invite you to enter the meadow. Small meadows in damper regions, prairies in drier ones, chaparrals in the Pacific Southwest, and woodland edges in the Northeast work as transitional zones between formal lawns and property boundaries.

Fall Color and Winter Interest

Winter is the true test of a garden and a good time to plan and make design and planting changes. Flaws of design are exposed when there are no leaves or blossoms to camouflage them. In northern gardens, use the features of your garden—walls, fences, and gateways; steps and walks, contouring of the ground; and shapes of planting beds and lawn areas—to give structure. The details of paving patterns, water features, sculpture, and handsome containers take on new visual interest. Bare branches and evergreens covered with frost, snow, and ice shape even a leafless environment. In southern gardens most plants remain in leaf to reinforce the hard edges of the basic design, but here, too, weaknesses may be evident with the advent of colder weather. To avoid monotony, reject the too easy all-green garden and make the most of seasonal change opportunities. Plant winter-flowering magnolias, camellias, and fruit trees; precooled narcissus; and tulips. Include variegated plants and those with outstanding fall foliage colors.

Northern gardens go dormant slowly through the fall months and gradually adjust to the rigors of winter. Southern gardens, however, are subject to extreme temperature fluctuations to which they may not have had time to adjust. Select plants that are hardy in your zone and site them carefully to ensure their survival. Cover tender plants as necessary to protect from burning winter sun, dehydrating winds, and sudden frost.

Narrow the gap between the last blooms of fall and the first blooms of spring by creating or exploiting spots in the garden that are warmer than others—places where the winter sun strikes or the snow melts early. South-facing rock and masonry walls will absorb heat during the day and radiate it back at night. Areas protected from wind will be warmer. Raised beds and soil that has been amended to be well drained will contain less water and reduce the likelihood of root rot. Avoid planting early-flowering shrubs and fruit trees in low-lying areas that collect cold air flows.

Window views gain importance as the weather turns cold and wet. Glimpses of a sunny pocket filled with the earliest blooming plants will lure you out for a stroll. In winter, plants seem less isolated and more appealing if they are tucked into a protected corner or set against a wall or evergreen background. Use plants with good form and interesting attributes. Even deciduous plants have a great diversity of growth habits: widespreading doublefile viburnum (*Viburnum* var. *tomentosum* 'Mariesii'), upright star magnolia (*M. stellata*), or low and spreading stephanandra (*Stephanandra incisa*), and cotoneaster.

In northern gardens, there are few winter-flowering shrubs, but they are extremely fragrant and deserving of a protected spot. Among them are wintersweet (*Chimonanthus praecox*), winter honeysuckle (*Lonicera fragrantissima*), winter hazel (*Corylopsis pauciflora*), and early-blooming Korean spice viburnum (*V. carlesii*). Other shrubs, such as witch hazel (*Hamamelis* spp.), bloom in fall and winter depending on variety, and leatherleaf mahonia (*Mahonia bealii, M. japonica*) and pieris (*Pieris japonica*) bridge the gap from winter to spring with drooping racemes of yellow or white flowers. Underplant these shrubs with clumps of Christmas and Lenten roses (*Helleborus nigra, H. orientalis*) and the earliest spring bulbs—species crocus (*C. sieberi, C. chrysanthus, C. susianus, C. tomasinianus*), snowdrops, and winter aconite.

Northeast
Frost is possible

Mid-Atlantic
Frost is possible

Mid-South
Frost is possible

Gulf & South Atlantic Coasts
Early frost is possible

Pacific Southwest & the Desert
Frost is possible

Pacific Northwest
Frost is possible

Rocky Mountains & the Plains
Frost is possible

GARDENING GUIDE ~ PLANTING

Northeast

OUTDOORS: Plant evergreens until mid-month, deciduous plants, tulips, lily bulbs until ground freezes. Continue potting up hardy, spring-blooming bulbs to force into bloom indoors.
INDOORS: Plant tazetta narcissus (paperwhite, 'Cragford', or 'Soleil d'Or') in pebbles and water for forcing. Groom house plants. Check frequently for insects and diseases.

Mid-Atlantic

OUTDOORS: Plant evergreens until mid-month, deciduous plants, tulips, lily bulbs until ground freezes. Continue potting up hardy, spring-blooming bulbs to force into bloom indoors. Store in unheated garage, basement, or well-mulched garden trench.
INDOORS: Plant hyacinths in a hyacinth glass for forcing.

Mid-South

OUTDOORS: Continue planting, transplanting deciduous and new and established evergreen trees and shrubs, roses. Continue dividing perennials, planting annuals. Finish planting early bulbs. Begin planting lilies, tulips, hyacinths. Sow cool-season vegetables in cold frame.

Gulf & South Atlantic Coasts

OUTDOORS: Continue planting, transplanting evergreens. Begin planting deciduous trees and shrubs after leaf fall, berries, figs, bare-root roses. Continue planting early spring-blooming bulbs, lilies, perennials. Plant cool-season annuals, winter vegetables to winter over. *Zone 9:* continue planting fruit and nut trees.

Pacific Southwest & the Desert

OUTDOORS: Begin planting, transplanting deciduous trees and shrubs, perennials. Continue planting fruit trees, berries, figs, grapes. Plant spring-blooming bulbs. Begin planting tulips, hyacinths. Continue dividing perennials, including ornamental grasses. Complete wildflower planting. *Zones 9, 8:* plant cool-season annuals; sow cool-season vegetables to winter over.

Pacific Northwest

OUTDOORS: Continue planting, transplanting deciduous plants if ground is friable. Finish planting spring-blooming bulbs. Continue dividing late perennials, ornamental grasses, water lilies. Sow sweet peas. Sow cool-season vegetables to winter over. Plant winter rye as cover crop. INDOORS: Plant tazetta narcissus in pebbles and water for forcing.

Rocky Mountains & the Plains

OUTDOORS: Plant evergreens until mid-month, deciduous plants, tulips, lilies until ground freezes. Continue potting up hardy, spring-blooming bulbs to force into bloom indoors.
INDOORS: Plant tazetta narcissus in pebbles and water, hyacinths in a hyacinth glass for forcing.

PRUNING

Northeast

Finish pruning late summer- and fall-blooming shrubs. Limit pruning of spring-flowering trees and shrubs to removal of awkward, diseased, or damaged branches to preserve bloom buds. Prune raspberry bushes. Trim ivy.

Mid-Atlantic

Prune late summer- and fall-blooming trees and shrubs. Limit pruning of spring-flowering plants to removal of awkward, damaged, or diseased branches to preserve bloom buds. Prune raspberries. Cut asparagus fronds to the ground. Call an arborist to check trees for susceptibility to storm damage. Trim ivy.

Mid-South

Prune newly planted and transplanted trees and shrubs to compensate for root loss. Limit pruning of spring-flowering plants to removal of awkward, diseased, or damaged branches to preserve bloom bud.

Gulf & South Atlantic Coasts

Prune and cut back newly planted trees, shrubs to compensate for root loss. Pinch back cool-season annuals to retard bloom and encourage stocky plants. Prune and fasten climbers against wind damage. Cut asparagus fronds to the ground.

Pacific Southwest & the Desert

Prune and cut back newly transplanted trees, shrubs to compensate for root loss. Pinch back cool-season annuals to prevent buds from forming early and being frost-nipped. Cut asparagus fronds to the ground.

Pacific Northwest

Prune and cut back newly transplanted plants to compensate for root loss.

Rocky Mountains & the Plains

Finish pruning late summer- and fall-blooming shrubs. Limit pruning of spring-flowering trees and shrubs to removal of awkward, dead, or diseased branches to save bloom buds. Trim ivy. Prune raspberry bushes. Cut asparagus fronds to the ground.

Fertilizing & Garden Highlights

Northeast

Fertilize trees, shrubs, and vines when fully dormant. Spray broadleaf and newly planted needle evergreens, rose canes with antidesiccant to prevent moisture loss.

Highlights. Broadleaf and needle evergreens; lingering fall color of fruit, berries, and foliage.

Mid-Atlantic

Fertilize deciduous and evergreen trees and shrubs when fully dormant. Fertilize raspberry bushes.

Highlights. Shrubs: sasanqua camellia, elaeagnus, wintersweet, witch hazel; fall color: lingering berries and fruits, foliage of broadleaf and needle evergreens and ground covers.

Mid-South

Fertilize deciduous and evergreen trees and shrubs, vines when fully dormant. Change or deepen hydrangea colors between now and January; treat pink ones with lime, blue with sulfate of ammonia.

Highlights. Perennials: chrysanthemum; shrubs: camellia, osmanthus, rose, witch hazel; trees: broadleaf and needle evergreens.

Gulf & South Atlantic Coasts

Finish fertilizing permanent plantings. Change or deepen hydrangea colors between now and January; treat pink ones with lime, blue with sulfate of ammonia.

Highlights. Fall-blooming annuals and perennials; shrubs: camellia, lantana, osmanthus, poinsettia, rose; trees: broadleaf and needle evergreens.

Pacific Southwest & the Desert

Complete fertilizing of woody plants. Feed cool-season annuals. Fumigate empty vegetable garden to control overwintering insects and diseases.

Highlights. Annuals: calendula, ornamental cabbage and kale, pansy, sunflower; perennials; shrubs; climbers; lingering fall fruits, berries, and color.

Pacific Northwest

Change or deepen hydrangea colors between now and January; treat pink ones with lime, blue with sulfate of ammonia. Spray broadleaf and newly planted needle evergreens with antidesiccant when temperature is above 40° to guard against moisture loss.

Highlights. Broadleaf and needle evergreens; lingering fall color.

Rocky Mountains & the Plains

Fertilize deciduous and evergreen trees and shrubs, raspberries when fully dormant to promote root growth. Spray broadleaf and newly planted evergreens, rose canes with antidesiccant when temperature is above 40°.

Highlights. Broadleaf and needle evergreens.

year _____

GARDEN MAINTENANCE

Northeast

Continue raking and composting leaves. Finish cleaning up beds. Cut perennial stalks to 4", except ornamental grasses, which add winter interest. Begin spreading winter mulches, preparing winter plant protection. Mow wildflower meadows. Feed birds. Lawn care: fertilize after first frost to promote root growth.

Mid-Atlantic

Prepare plants for winter. Heavily mulch roses. Water dogwood, broadleaf evergreens, newly planted trees thoroughly before ground freezes. Clean up perennial beds, cut stalks to 4". Mow wildflower meadows. Feed birds. Lawn care: fertilize after first frost to promote root growth; lime if necessary.

Mid-South

Mow wildflower meadows. Rake and compost leaves. Move tender plants to shelter. Mulch or cover marginal plants if frost threatens. Water evergreens thoroughly before ground freezes. Feed birds. Lawn care: fertilize after first frost to promote root growth; overseed warm-season grasses with annual winter rye.

Gulf & South Atlantic Coasts

Mow wildflower meadows. Cut perennial stalks to 4", except ornamental grasses, which add winter interest. Water newly planted and transplanted plants, bulb beds. Lawn care: keep grass cut going into winter; rake regularly; fertilize cool-season grasses for last time. *Zone 10:* check irrigation systems—prepare to water during dry season. Protect tender plants from quick freezes.

Pacific Southwest & the Desert

Rake up and compost leaves. Clean up, weed, shape, edge beds. Begin winter protection from quick freezes for tender plants. Remove covers as temperatures rise. Continue to water (including citrus) until winter rains begin. Lawn care: keep grass cut going into winter; feed cool-season grasses to promote root growth.

Pacific Northwest

Mow wildflower meadows. Protect tender plants from quick freezes. Remove covers as temperatures rise. Move tender container plants to protected areas. Water evergreens thoroughly before ground freezes. Lawn care: keep grass cut going into winter; rake; feed cool-season grasses to promote root growth.

Rocky Mountains & the Plains

Keep leaves raked and composted. Mow wildflower meadows. Protect tender plants from winter damage with guy wires, tree wrap, burlap windscreens, mulches. Mulch roses heavily after ground freezes. Feed birds. Lawn care: fertilize after first frost to promote root growth.

DESIGNING FOR FALL COLOR AND WINTER INTEREST

Many annuals and perennials will continue to add color until frost—aster, chrysanthemum, Japanese anemone, calamintha, tricyrtis, campanula, dianthus, cleome, marigold, salvia, ornamental cabbage and kale, sedums and ornamental grasses. They are joined by fall-flowering bulbs—crocus, colchicum, lycoris, nerine, and cyclamen. Behind this, as temperatures drop, deciduous trees and shrubs are beginning to turn. Maples, ash, Callery pear, kadsura, sourwood (*Oxydendron arboreum*), sour gum (*Nyssa sylvatica*), sweet gum (*Liquidambar styraciflua*), ginkgo, oaks, aspen, smokebush (*Cotinus coggygria*), shadbush (*Amelanchier sp.*), sumac, winged euonymus (*E. alata*), fothergilla, Virginia sweetspire (*Itea virginica*), franklinia, and deciduous azaleas are among the most colorful.

Summer-flowering shrubs continue to bloom into fall. Hydrangeas are outstanding for variety and richness—lace-cap (*H. macrophylla*) with wide, flat, lacy blooms beginning to dry, Peegee (*H. paniculata* var. 'Grandiflora'), with white tapering blooms turning slowly pink, and shade-tolerant oakleaf (*H. quercifolia*), with white pyramidal blooms that turn purplish and dry well for flower arrangements. Still to come are the autumn colors of its scalloped oakleaf-shaped leaves—crimson, orange, and purple.

Hypericum has been producing single clear-yellow blossoms since early summer. Potentilla is still blooming profusely in yellows, whites, and soft orange. After leaf fall, its dense twiggy structure and warm brown bark will add color to a mixed shrub border along with low evergreen ornamental grasses. The long, tapering leaves of butterfly bush (*Buddleia* spp.) flash silvery in a breeze, and its scented blossoms in white, lavender, and purple are irresistible to butterflies. Two shrubs without character in other seasons but outstanding for colorful blossoms in the fall garden are althaea *(Hibiscus syriacus)*, with its hollyhocklike blossoms, and hardy fuchsias, with dangling red and purple blossoms. They need to be carefully integrated into a mixed border and visually supported by shrubs with stronger foliage, or softly pruned into hedges.

As ground covers or under planting for taller shrubs, heathers and heaths bring muted but contrasting colors—green against yellow, gray against red and orange—to add to the autumn scene. They look good in a grouping on a hillside with lowbush blueberries and dwarf needle evergreens to which fall-blooming bulbs can be added.

After leaf fall, the bare branches of deciduous plants continue to provide a framework. The sky is dramatized by the silhouettes of sycamore and oak or a row of poplars. Catkins dangle on hazels and alders. Deciduous vines decorate masonry walls with their branching patterns. And there is the additional interest of newly exposed

bark—green-stemmed broom *(Cistus praecox)* and *kerria (K. japonica)*, red-twig dogwood *(Cornus sericea)*, yellow-twig dogwood *(C. sericea* var. 'Flaviramea'), exfoliating cornelian cherry *(C. mas)*, Oriental dogwood *(C. kousa)*, crape myrtle *(Lagerstroemia indica)*, and eucalyptus, paper birch, and paperbark maple *(Acer griseum)*.

But it is the evergreens with their specific shapes that take on new importance as focal points or backdrops for other plants. Against this basic structure, plants chosen for their year-round qualities may be added to bring about a continuing series of events.

In warm climates the list of winter-blooming shrubs and trees is longer, with fall- and winter-blooming *camellias (C. sasanqua, C. japonica, C. reticulata)*, cassias, poinsettias, silk-tassel *(Garrya elliptica)*, winter jasmine and daphne, star magnolia and early evergreen Kurume and indica azaleas. With these come early bulbs and winter hardy annuals, calendula, sweet alyssum, sweet peas, stock, hollyhocks, petunias, and pansies and poppies seeded in the fall.

Berries enliven the fall garden and provide food for wildlife.

HOUSE PLANTS FOR ALL SEASONS

Ever since the nineteenth century and the advent of the heated glass conservatory, growing plants indoors as decorative elements has ranged from a hobby to a passion. The great influx of new plants brought back to England by Victorian botanical explorers from the tropics, the deserts, and alpine slopes were first displayed in greenhouses, conservatories, and winter gardens. They began moving into the house proper when it was discovered that many would grow under much less specialized conditions, and that home environments could be altered to suit them. The term house plants was born.

For would-be gardeners with a longing to grow things but without soil in which to dig, gardening indoors has a special meaning. Gardening on windowsills, under skylights, in solar spaces, under artificial lights in dim apartments or basements, or in greenhouses presents new challenges and gives great pleasure. There is much to be said for watching the unfolding of a cymbidium or an amaryllis, the charm of a clerodendrum, jasmine, or abutilon in bloom, or the brilliant color of a lily on the windowsill with a snowy

Northeast
Winter conditions prevail

Mid-Atlantic
Winter conditions prevail

Mid-South
Frost is possible

Gulf & South Atlantic Coasts
Frost is possible

Pacific Southwest & the Desert
Frost is possible

Pacific Northwest
Frost is possible

Rocky Mountains & the Plains
Winter conditions prevail

field beyond. Practical matters such as heat conservation, which has lowered household temperatures, and the high cost of cut flowers may in part be responsible for the current interest in and expanded possibilities of indoor gardening.

In areas of the country where winter comes early and spring comes late, indoor gardening extends the growing season. There are traditional housebound plants—aspidistra, palms, philodendron, schefflera, and ferns—and some tender garden plants—geraniums and such herbs as rosemary or bay—that have long wintered indoors. Combined on a sunny windowsill with a mass display of flowering bulbs, this "garden" can brighten any late-winter day. Many unusual species of tulip and crocus can be forced along with the traditional narcissus, hyacinth, freesia, and amaryllis. The addition of a few branches of pussy willow, forsythia, or quince helps to enhance a room until the arrival of spring.

In regions of the country where favorite ornamental plants are marginally hardy, gardening in a cool greenhouse or garden room gives tender, temperate camellias; some azaleas; and tropical plants—gardenias, hibiscus, palms, oleander, bananas, gingers, heliconias, and plumerias—protection from extreme winter temperatures and early or late frosts.

GARDENING GUIDE ~ PLANTING

Northeast
INDOORS: Continue planting narcissus at two-week intervals for continuous bloom. Check house plants frequently, groom well, wash off or spray insect problems. Turn plants regularly in window for even development.

Mid-Atlantic
INDOORS: Continue planting narcissus at two-week intervals for continuous bloom. Give holiday-flowering plants proper care: water, feed, provide correct day and night temperatures, protect from drafts and cold windows.

Mid-South
OUTDOORS: Finish planting trees, shrubs, tulips, hyacinths. Finish transplanting roses. *Lower South:* sow cool-season vegetables and salad greens in cold frame. INDOORS: Start tazetta narcissus (paperwhite, 'Cragford', 'Soleil d'Or') in pebbles and water. Give holiday-flowering plants proper care: water, feed, provide correct day and night temperatures.

Gulf & South Atlantic Coasts
OUTDOORS: Continue planting, transplanting deciduous trees and shrubs, vines, fruits (including citrus), nuts, figs, grapes, roses, asparagus when ground is friable. Finish planting early spring-flowering bulbs and lilies. Begin planting tulips and hyacinths. Sow cool-season vegetables.

Pacific Southwest & the Desert
OUTDOORS: Finish planting, transplanting deciduous and evergreen trees and shrubs, roses while dormant. Plant bare-root fruit and nut trees, berries, grapes. Finish planting spring-blooming bulbs, winter annuals, perennials. *Zone 10:* sow cool-season vegetables in cold frame. *Zones 10, 9:* start warm-season vegetables in flats indoors.

Pacific Northwest
OUTDOORS: Finish planting, transplanting deciduous and evergreen trees and shrubs, vines, roses, perennials, spring-blooming bulbs, cool-season annuals. INDOORS: Continue planting narcissus at two-week intervals for continuous bloom.

Rocky Mountains & the Plains
INDOORS: Continue planting narcissus at two-week intervals for continuous bloom indoors. Give holiday-flowering plants proper care. Check house plants frequently, groom well, treat insect and disease problems promptly. Protect plants from drafts and icy windows. Turn regularly for even development.

year _____

year _____

PRUNING

Northeast

Gather greens from the garden for holiday decorations indoors. Mix broadleaf and needle evergreens, berries, climbers, ground covers. Add interesting berries, pinecones, seedpods. Cut winter- and early spring-blooming shrubs to force into bloom indoors.

Mid-Atlantic

Prune carefully for holiday greens from the garden. Gather broadleaf and needle evergreens, deciduous and evergreen vines to wind into wreaths. Add ground covers, interesting berries, cones, seedpods. Cut winter- and spring-blooming shrubs to force into bloom indoors.

Mid-South

Prune deciduous trees, summer- and fall-blooming shrubs after leaf fall when fully dormant. Prune berry bushes, grape and other deciduous vines when leaf fall reveals structure. Gather holiday greens. Mix broadleaf and needle evergreens, ground covers. Add interesting berries, cones, seedpods.

Gulf & South Atlantic Coasts

Gather holiday greens from the garden. Cut chrysanthemums to 3" after bloom. Deadhead annuals. *Zone 10:* prune root-hardy tropicals that have suffered frost damage. *Zone 9:* prune established deciduous and evergreen trees, shrubs, vines while dormant, and new plants to compensate for root loss.

Pacific Southwest & the Desert

Prune established deciduous and evergreen trees, shrubs, vines, ground covers while dormant. Call an arborist for major tree work. Gather holiday greens from the garden. Mix broadleaf and needle evergreens, berries, cones, seedpods. *Zone 10:* prune root-hardy tropicals that have suffered frost damage.

Pacific Northwest

Prune fruit and nut trees, berry bushes, grape and other vines when leaf fall has revealed branching structure. Gather holiday greens from the garden. Mix broadleaf and needle evergreens, ground covers. Cut evergreen and deciduous vines to wind into wreaths. Add interesting berries, cones, seedpods.

Rocky Mountains & the Plains

Gather holiday greens from the garden. Mix broadleaf and needle evergreens, ground covers, deciduous and evergreen vines. Add interesting berries, cones, seedpods. Cut branches from winter- and early spring-flowering shrubs and trees to force into bloom indoors.

FERTILIZING & GARDEN HIGHLIGHTS

Northeast

Watch for overwintering insects and diseases.

Highlights. Lingering berries, buds, and pods: dogwood, ornamental grasses, paulownia, sophora, sweet gum, sycamore; plant silhouettes: birch, elm, ginkgo, oak, poplar, willow.

Mid-Atlantic

Watch for overwintering insects and diseases.

Highlights. Fall color: berries—Christmasberry, hawthorn, holly, nandina, pyracantha, stranvaesia; evergreens—hemlock, junipers, pine, spruce, yew; winter interest: buds, pods, bark, plant silhouettes.

Mid-South

Fertilize winter-blooming annuals. Watch for overwintering insects and diseases.

Highlights. Bulbs: early crocus, hardy cyclamen, daffodil; perennials: hellebore; shrubs: camellia, osmanthus, wintersweet, witch hazel.

Gulf & South Atlantic Coasts

Fertilize winter-blooming annuals, emerging bulbs, vegetable seedlings. Spray vacant vegetable gardens with fumigant to kill insects and diseases.

Highlights. Bulbs: amaryllis, calla lily, early narcissus; annuals: ornamental cabbage and kale, violet, sweet pea; shrubs: camellia, poinsettia, rose.

Pacific Southwest & the Desert

Fertilize winter-blooming annuals, emerging spring bulbs. Treat azaleas, camellias with iron chelate if necessary. Spray rose canes with antidesiccant.

Highlights. Bulbs: clivia; hardy annuals; shrubs: azalea, camellia, erica, grevillea, melaleuca, pernettya.

Pacific Northwest

Fertilize winter-blooming annuals, emerging bulbs, vegetable seedlings.

Highlights. Winter interest: buds and pods—catalpa, dogwood, goldenrain tree, magnolia, sycamore; bark—cherry, crape myrtle, Oriental dogwood, lacebark pine, maple, stewartia; plant silhouettes—birch, corkscrew willow, ginkgo, poplar.

Rocky Mountains & the Plains

Spray broadleaf and newly planted evergreens with antidesiccant if not done in late fall.

Highlights. Indoor bloom: bulbs—amaryllis, crocus, hyacinth, lily of the valley, narcissus, tulip; house plants—African violet, Christmas cactus, cyclamen, orchid, poinsettia.

year _____

GARDEN MAINTENANCE

Northeast

Finish fall cleanup and winter plant protection. After ground freezes, mulch bulb beds, perennials, other small plants. Set tree guards to protect tender ornamentals, apples, cherries from rodent damage. Ventilate cold frames until ground freezes, then cover lightly. Feed birds.

Mid-Atlantic

Finish fall cleanup, winter plant protection. After ground freezes, mulch small plants to prevent frost heave and sunscald. To prevent indelible footprints, do not walk on frozen grass. Check hardy bulbs potted up earlier for dryness and root development. Clean and sharpen garden tools. Feed birds.

Mid-South

Clean up beds. Pull frosted annuals. Mulch trees, shrubs, perennials, bulbs after hard frost 4"–6". Water newly planted plants and bulb beds if season is dry. Clean, oil, sharpen, and store tools. Service mowers and spray equipment. Feed birds. Lawn care: rake leaves before they mat, apply pre-emergent weed control.

Gulf & South Atlantic Coasts

Rake leaves. Pull spent plants. Mulch established and newly planted plants, roses. Provide winter plant protection for tender plants: cover or move to sheltered spot if frost threatens; water regularly to prevent frost damage. Lawn care: fertilize cool-season grasses, winter rye; start weed control.

Pacific Southwest & the Desert

Rake and compost leaves. Pull spent plants. Cultivate beds. Mulch newly planted and established plants. Move marginally hardy plants to protected area. Continue to water every two weeks in dry areas. Service irrigation systems. Lawn care: fertilize cool-season grasses, winter rye; start weed control.

Pacific Northwest

Keep leaves raked and composted. Finish fall cleanup of beds. Pull all spent plants. Cultivate lightly before ground freezes. Mulch all trees, shrubs, perennials after first hard frost. Water newly planted and broadleaf evergreens, bulb beds if season is dry. Protect marginally hardy plants.

Rocky Mountains & the Plains

Finish fall cleanup, winter plant protection. Set snow fences. After ground freezes, mulch bulb beds, perennials, other small plants to prevent heaving during periods of thawing and freezing. Set tree guards against rodent damage. Wrap tender trunks against sunscald. Continue to water every few weeks on warm days if season is dry. Feed birds.

year _____

year _____

DESIGNING WITH HOUSE PLANTS

Success in designing with house plants comes from knowing how to grow them properly and use them effectively.

Growing house plants requires knowing as much as possible about their native habitats and trying to replicate those conditions of light, humidity, and day- and nighttime temperatures. Use of a handheld light meter and knowledge of the minimum light requirements of the plants you want to grow are essential. A low-light situation can be modified with additional light from grow lights, fluorescent tubes, or mercury-vapor lamps. In addition, climates vary within the house, from cool, drafty entrance halls and bright but often dry living and family rooms, to moist, steamy kitchens and bathrooms, or unheated sunny conservatories where the temperatures may drop 10 degrees or more at night. These are microclimates and are as significant as those in the outdoor garden. They can be modified somewhat; an analysis of the site and growing conditions will determine how you should proceed.

Designing with house plants requires a careful scrutiny of the style of the setting and the choice of plants and planters whose decorative qualities will enhance and blend with it. Texture, form, scale, and color are as relevant indoors as out.

The bold forms of tropical plants suit contemporary architecture. Stark settings can be softened and vast spaces united with large weeping figs *(Ficus benjamina)* or fishtail palms. In a rustic country setting, more delicate violets, miniature roses, and scented and zonal geraniums are appropriate. Podocarpus, Ming aralia, and bamboo harmonize with an Oriental setting. In a period setting, one beautifully groomed plant or a collection of plants in a well-lighted corner or bay window has more impact than a disorderly scattering of different plants around the room.

Set a different mood at night. Spotlighting plants on a table or shelf, backlighting or sidelighting an outstanding leaf pattern, or silhouetting a group of plants against a wall can create a dramatic effect. Careful use of soft lighting reveals warm and delicate flower colors.

Containers should not distract from the plants they hold; they should not compete with the colors of the plants and should be in scale with them. Avoid an overwhelmed or pinched look. Choose a container that is suitable both practically and aesthetically for its setting. A large terracotta pot can contain a multistemmed false aralia; a classic urn sets off a cascading Boston fern; a simple flaring vase flatters a spreading foliage plant; a basket with a handle provides a hold for a small climbing vine; a classic Versailles box sets off a standard, upright, clipped bay tree. When grouping plants with diverse shapes and textures, put them in pots of similar style and color to provide unity to the design. Or conversely, use the same-shaped plant in containers of different styles.

In low-light areas, an inner-office space, a front hall, or an elevator lobby, try a terrarium—a small greenhouse with controlled humidity and protection from drafts. Include a built-in fluorescent tube. A terrarium, or Wardian case, can house a world of miniature plants: dwarf palms, mosses, violets, begonias, fittonia, and orchids.

Under a skylighted stairwell or on a well-lighted staircase landing, group foliage plants such as aspidistra, fatshedera, and false aralia. If height is a consideration, place low plants on stands, brackets, or tabletops.

For a bright conservatory, choose plants demanding sunlight in winter: amaryllis, geraniums, begonias, dwarf citrus, flowering maple. They can be staged or raised on steps of different levels in front of the windowsill. They provide a dazzling display of color. If the room is cool and nighttime temperatures fall by 10 degrees, gardenias, jade trees, camellias, sweet olive, and many orchids will also bloom. Once in bloom, however, the blossoms will last longer if kept out of direct sunlight. Also remember that sunlight will strengthen as spring approaches, and plants may need to be drawn back or shaded to protect them from too much heat or sun.

Still in the conservatory, but farther away from the windows, spathiphyllum, fuchsias, bromeliads, African violets, kalanchoe, and kohleria will flower, and many foliage plants will flourish as a background. Ferns and cyperus growing in water in a handsome pot make a nice contrast when they loft over a collection of Christmas cactus and cineraria, or impatiens, geraniums, and coleus grown from cuttings taken from the garden in late summer.

In the kitchen an arrangement of glass shelves in a light-filled window can hold a collection of favorite plants. Try succulents planted in matching pots or herbs started from seed or potted up from the summer garden to be used fresh by the cook.

As useful as plants are for softening interior architecture and uniting and defining space, they add the most excitement by bringing seasonal color and life indoors in the winter. Poinsettias, cyclamen, and orchids are to winter as primroses, hyacinths, and clivia are to spring and chrysanthemums, tuberous begonias, and flowering cactus are to fall.

Orchids are a welcome gift.

Gerber daisies are long-lasting cut flowers and bloom even longer in a pot.

PLANTING

Gardening is much easier if you put the right plant in the right place and plant it correctly. Knowing something about a plant's native habitat and the conditions to which it is adapted will enable you to understand its requirements. Some plants are fussy, but most are tolerant of a wide range of conditions. Consider the following site conditions:

light: sunny to shady
moisture: wet to dry
soil: clay to sand
nutrients: rich to poor
pH: acid to alkaline

Study seed and plant catalogs carefully to select special plants for special situations, such as acid or alkaline soil or boggy or dry spots. Choose disease-resistant and proven varieties or those recommended by your local Cooperative Extension Service. Try native plants for easy maintenance and to reduce spraying for insects and disease.

❦ How to prepare the soil

TEST FOR AND AMEND SOIL STRUCTURE

In planting beds. Pick up a handful of soil. It should form a ball easily and fall apart readily when dropped. Good gardening soil should be of the proper texture, or friability, to allow the slow, steady passage of water and nutrients to the root zone. Amend heavy clay soils with sharp sand, gypsum, and organic material (compost, leaf mold, aged manure, and if a more acid soil is needed, dampened peat moss) by as much as one-third. Amend light, sandy soil with organic materials and humus by as much as half. Protect soil structure by not working wet, soggy soil. Planting in soil that is too wet will compact it and rot seeds and seedlings. Always dig deeply, and turn and mix in amendments well. Prepare planting areas in the fall if possible so the ground has a chance to settle over the winter. If not, allow a week or two in advance of planting.

In the vegetable garden. Prepare planting areas in the fall, if possible, to give the ground a chance to settle over the winter. In the spring, test the soil. Adjust the pH if necessary. Amend with manure, leafy compost, or other organic material and spade in. Cultivate to a depth of 12 inches when the ground is dry enough to work. Level the area by raking and let the soil settle for a few weeks. Most vegetables prefer a rich, well-drained, neutral soil (6.0–7.5). When preparing the vegetable garden in the spring, mix in a granular fertilizer (5-10-5 and 10-10-10) along with 2–3 inches of aged manure, compost, or leaf mold.

TEST FOR DRAINAGE

Fill a planting hole with water. The water should leave a well-drained hole in ten minutes. If it takes thirty minutes or more, the soil requires correction. In areas with shallow soil or a high water table, plant high by elevating the existing soil level with raised beds or by mounding the soil under the plants. Correct surface drainage to ensure that rainwater does not sit in low spots.

❦ How to choose plants

Select only healthy plants from a reliable source, preferably a grower in your region, to ensure hardiness and adaptability to your climate and soil. Buy the largest plant you can afford so you have a show the first year. Always buy nursery-grown stock—avoid plants collected from the wild—and make sure the nursery gives a guarantee; the standard one is for a year when the nursery installs a major tree or shrub. Purchasing mail-order plants is a gamble unless you check carefully to be sure they will do well in your area.

Trees, shrubs, and other smaller plants are sold bare-root, ball-and-burlapped (b & b), or in containers. A bare-root plant is sold in a dormant condition only in late winter. A b & b plant is grown in a field, dug out in early spring, and wrapped in burlap to keep the dirt intact and protect the roots from drying out. A container-grown plant is grown in a container that keeps the root systems intact.

TREES

Large trees are commonly sold b & b. Smaller trees may be available either bare-root or container-grown. Select an average tree within any size group. An overgrown specimen will suffer a greater leaf loss when pruned back to compensate for root loss. A smaller tree may never attain vigorous growth. Choose a tree with a vertical, well-balanced, and even branching habit. Be sure the main leader has not been pruned out. Look for a balance between the top, or head, and the root ball. A well-balanced tree will establish more readily. The root system should be evenly developed and symmetrical. Avoid a tree with kinked or encircling roots visible on the soil surface. If the tree is in leaf, leaf color should be dark and even, not scorched or yellowed.

Bare-root. Bare-root trees are less expensive than container-grown or b & b ones. Select a bare-root tree as soon as this stock is available in nurseries. Fruit trees are commonly available when bare-root. Look for a tree with undamaged roots radiating evenly out from the trunk. Plant it within a day or two, or pack the roots carefully in moist peat moss or sawdust and set it in the shade until it can be planted. A bare-root tree can also be stored "heeled in" (buried up to the tips) in a trench or kept damp and cool for several weeks. Never let the roots dry out.

Balled-and-burlapped. B & b trees can be planted whenever available, but preferably in the spring or fall. The root ball, or soil ball, should be compact and firm, not cracked or broken. A firm root ball indicates a well-developed, fibrous root system that is able to support the tree. Until planting time, shade the tree, keep the root ball moist by carefully watering with a slow hose from the top, and occasionally spray the foliage.

Container-grown. Container-grown trees may be planted as available during the growing season. Check that a staked tree has a strong trunk by untying it. Reject it if the stem does not remain straight. Until planting time, either set the container in the shade or cover it with peat moss or soil. Keep the root ball moist and occasionally spray the foliage.

SHRUBS
Shrubs are most commonly sold in containers, but they may also be purchased b & b or bare-root. Select a shrub that is evenly developed with a well-balanced branching habit and even form. Reject a plant with blunt, stubbily pruned ends or crossing branches, which invite insects and diseases.

Bare-root. Bare-root shrubs are less expensive than container-grown and b & b shrubs and are available only when dormant. Choose a plant with firm roots that radiate evenly and at different levels out from the main root to anchor the plant and ensure symmetrical growth. Do not allow roots to dry out. Plant as soon as possible and before growth begins.

Balled-and-burlapped. Plant b & b shrubs when available, but preferably in the spring or fall. Look for a well-developed, fibrous root system. Reject a shrub with a dry, cracked, or loose root ball. Push your finger into the top several inches of dirt near the trunk to see whether it has encircling or kinked roots. Until planting time, shade the shrub, keep the soil moist, and spray the foliage occasionally.

Container-grown. Select a container-grown shrub that is well anchored in its container. To test, lift carefully by the trunk. If the soil moves too easily, the shrub probably has an undeveloped root system, having recently been moved from a smaller container. Conversely, if there is a thick mass of roots visible on the soil surface and around the edge of the root ball, the plant has been in the container too long and may be rootbound and unable to recover when transplanted. Reject a plant in a rusted, split, or disintegrating container, which may indicate that the roots have grown out into the soil at the nursery and will result in shock to the plant when moved. Until planting time, shade the container because hot sun will heat up the roots, especially in a metal can. Keep the root ball moist and spray the foliage occasionally.

BULBS AND TUBERS
Bulbs should be firm and unblemished and should feel heavy for their size. The heaviness indicates that they have not dried out.

PERENNIALS AND SEEDLINGS
Choose healthy-looking plants. Check that the stems are short and thick. Tall, lanky plants will have weak root systems. Avoid plants that have yellow or discolored foliage, or whose roots have grown out of the container. Inspect for insects and disease.

❦ How to plant

TREES AND SHRUBS
Measure the size of the root ball to eliminate guesswork. Place a piece of burlap to the side of the hole to hold the soil. Dig a hole twice as wide as the root ball and of the same depth—or a little shallower because the plant may sink slightly. Set the plant carefully. Stand back to check the placement and straightness. Backfill the hole, tamping the dirt down lightly with your foot or the shovel as you go. Build a shallow saucer of dirt around the base of the plant to hold water. Water thoroughly, using a slow hose until the soil is loose and muddy, to eliminate air pockets. Be sure to set the crown of the plant (the spot where the leafy top and the roots of the plant

meet) at the same depth at which it was originally growing. There is usually a visible soil line on the stem. If set too deep, the plant will drown. If set too shallow, the plant will dry out and die. (Slow-release fertilizer tablets may be dropped in the planting hole at planting time.)

Transplanting. Using a sharp spade, dig as large a root ball as possible. Lift and carry small plants on the spade. Tip large plants to one side of the hole, push a wad of burlap down one side, and pull under and around the ball. Wrap and tie the root ball securely. Lift the plant out onto a piece of plastic or cardboard and slide it to the new location. Minimize transplanting shock by moving plants when inactive or dormant and on cloudy days. Spray leafy plants with an antidesiccant to reduce moisture loss from leaves. Keep the root system moist, mist the foliage, and water (when out of the sunlight), or spray with antidesiccant. Prune the top back slightly to compensate for root loss.

Bare-root. Plant as soon as the soil is workable. Soak roots for several hours in tepid water before planting and prune any damaged roots or canes. Mound dirt in the center of a prepared hole and spread the roots over the mound. (Set a rose graft 1–2 inches below the surface.) Start adding soil carefully. Water in well when the hole is two-thirds filled. Finish filling the hole and firm the dirt gently around roots. Water in again. Mound loose dirt around the stem up to the lowest branch to protect the stem and steady the plant until it is established and leafed out. Then carefully remove the excess dirt and spread the mulch.

Balled-and-burlapped. Lift by grasping the burlap and cord, not the stem or trunk (which will tear roots). Set the plant in the hole, cut away cords, and tuck the burlap down into the planting hole, where it will rot. Remove plastic cord and wrapping, which will not rot.

Container-grown. Dig a hole wider than the container. Dampen the root ball in advance or cut the container down both sides to remove the plant. Check the root ball; cut the encircling roots, and untangle and spread out the matted roots. When the hole is partially filled, water in to eliminate air pockets. Fill the rest of the hole and pack soil gently. Water again and mulch. Thin out or trim the top of the plant back slightly to compensate for root loss.

PERENNIALS

Perennials are herbaceous plants that live and flower for three or more years where climate and gardening conditions are suitable. Their leafy tops die back to the ground in the winter, but the roots live on underground. In new flower borders, prepare the entire planting area in advance. Let the bed sit seven to ten days before planting. Plants can also be added to existing beds. In either case, dig a spacious hole for each plant and space them at recommended intervals. Set each plant at the same soil level at which it was growing before, especially those growing from a crown, such as pansies, Siberian iris,

astilbe, and phlox. Firm the soil gently and soak each plant until a puddle forms. Water seedlings in with a dilute solution of water-soluble fertilizer or manure tea.

WATER LILIES AND OTHER AQUATIC PLANTS

Wait for the water temperature to reach 70°. In a pail or basket, plant aquatic plants in soil mix (three parts heavy clay soil and one part dehydrated cow manure). Cover the soil surface with 1/2 inch of gravel to weight it down. Set the container in the pool with the soil surface 6–12 inches below the water surface. If the pool is very deep, create a platform for the container out of concrete blocks or bricks. Hardy water lilies and lotus are perennials that can remain in outdoor pools all year. Tropical water lilies are annuals and should be pulled and composted at the end of the season. Plan to renew the soil in the containers every second year.

IN A CONTAINER

Select a container that provides insulation (wood and fiberglass do; metal does not). Make sure there are adequate drainage holes. Add a 2-inch layer of pebbles, gravel, or pot shards to increase good drainage. Cover it with a piece of soil separator to prevent soil leakage. Fill the container with commercial potting soil mix, which drains well but retains moisture long enough for the roots to absorb it. Or mix your own potting soil: one part each topsoil, peat moss, perlite, and dehydrated cow manure. Add additional topsoil, up to a third for stability if planting small trees or a shrub. Mix well; just before planting, stir in three or four trowelsful of 5-10-5 granular fertilizer per bucket of soil. When planting vegetables, herbs, or annuals, add an

equal amount of bonemeal or horticultural limestone. Refurbish soil in an established container by adding granular 5-10-5 fertilizer and bonemeal, additional peat moss, or compost. Mix well.

When planting in containers, consider the ultimate sizes of the plants and the size, shape, and color of the foliage and blooms. Group together plants with similar cultural requirements (sun, shade, dryness, moisture). Harmonize the planter with its background. Select plants suitable for a colder climate (two zones farther north) to ensure winter-hardiness.

IN A HANGING BASKET

Set the wire basket in a large flower pot or bucket to steady it. Line the basket with 1-inch-thick, dampened spaghnum moss, and fill the center with good potting soil. Poke holes through the moss at the sides, and place plants through the holes into the soil. Next, plant the central section of the basket. Firm in well. Water in seedlings with a dilute solution of water-soluble fertilizer. Keep moss moistened at all times to provide humid air, because hanging baskets are highly exposed to wind and sun. Pinch back developing shoots to create a shapely and bushy plant.

BULBS OUTDOORS

Most bulbs prefer a sandy, well-drained soil. Avoid heavy clay or hardpan because poor drainage and excessive moisture, especially in winter, cause rot. Ensure good drainage by adding well-rotted compost, other organic matter, and sharp sand before planting, or plant in raised beds. Prepare bulb beds in advance and allow them to rest for several weeks before planting. If planting a large number of bulbs, excavate the entire area and enrich the soil. Bulbs can also be planted in individual holes in an existing bed. For both methods, add bonemeal or superphosphate to the soil at the bottom of each planting hole where the roots can easily reach it. Measure the depth of the planting hole from the top of the bulb to the soil surface. As a general rule, plant each bulb at a depth of two to three times its diameter and space one and a half to three times the planting depth. Plant bulbs in wire cages in the ground if your garden has rodent problems. Plant bulbs with their pointed ends upward. Mulch and water well. In containers, plant closely but do not let bulbs touch. Plant bulbs as soon as possible because they lose viability the longer they are out of the ground. If necessary, store in a cool place, such as the refrigerator, in paper bags, until you are ready to plant.

BULBS FOR FORCING

Bulbs can be forced indoors for continuous winter bloom. Plant them at two-week intervals to lengthen the blooming season, and try early and late varieties.

In dirt. Plant bulbs from early to late fall. Choose containers that drain well. Cover the holes with window screening or pot shards

and fill partially with soil mix. Use a commercial planting mix or a mixture of equal parts garden loam, coarse sand, and peat moss or ground bark. Set bulbs so that the tips are level with the container rim. Add soil until the bulbs are barely covered. Water well to settle. Place in a cool, protected spot until the bulbs root in fourteen to fifteen weeks. Containers can also be set in a trench in the garden and covered with a thick leaf or straw mulch to prevent freezing. Keep evenly moist. When bulbs are well rooted and sprouts are showing green (six to eight weeks), bring the container into warmth (60°) and light for an additional three to four weeks to force bloom.

In pebbles and water. Plant precooled bulbs from fall through early winter. Fill two-thirds of a shallow bowl with pebbles. Set narcissus bulbs barely touching with their flat sides toward the rim; start a Dutch hyacinth in a hyacinth glass. Add water until it barely touches the base of the bulbs. Place the containers in a cool, dark spot for a few weeks until roots develop and leaves appear. Then bring them into warmth and light. Maintain the water level through flowering. Compost the spent bulbs; they will not bloom again.

TUBERS

Before planting tubers, remove the largest eye to encourage a bushier plant. Plant tubers 1 inch deep on their sides with eyes up, in flats with a soil mix of equal parts moist sphagnum moss, compost, and sharp sand. Add superphosphate or bulb food, water well, and keep at 75°. When small leaves have formed, plant in the garden 1 inch deep at intervals of 8 inches for best coverage.

ANNUALS AND VEGETABLES FROM SEED

Read the instructions on the seed package for germination periods and requirements, transplanting times, and other pertinent information. To avoid leggy and overgrown seedlings, add the hardening-off period to the germination and growing times, and start seeds according to the last frost date in your region.

Sowing indoors. Fill a flat with moistened, commercially prepared, sterilized seed-starting mix. Mix small seeds with sand to ensure even distribution. Broadcast or sow the seeds in shallow furrows. Tiny seeds will fall in the crevices. Cover larger seeds with fine soil or vermiculite. Mist gently if the soil has dried out. Label each flat with the name of the plant and the date sown. Because germination times differ, plant only one kind of seed in each flat. To create a small greenhouse, place a plant label at each corner of the flat and slip the flat into a plastic bag, or cover the flat with a piece of glass or plastic wrap. Place it out of direct light. If condensation appears, open the flat and air the plant for several hours to avoid rot. Remove the cover when the first true leaves appear. Move the flat to indirect sunlight. Thin seedlings in their flat or prick out with a pencil point or tip of a label and transplant to individual containers. Fertilize every two weeks with water-soluble 20-20-20 fertilizer.

HARDENING OFF: Seedlings grown indoors or purchased from the greenhouse or garden center should be conditioned before being planted in the garden. To acclimatize seedlings to greater fluctuations of temperature and light, set them in a cold frame for seven to ten days, or set flats outside in a protected spot for an hour the first day and gradually lengthen the time each day thereafter.

Transplanting seedlings to the garden. Transplant seedlings when they fill their containers but before they become top-heavy or begin blooming. If the soil is dry, thoroughly dampen it in the planting bed a day in advance. Moisten the seedlings, or transplants, before removing them from the container. Run a knife around the rim on the inside and tap the container sharply on a hard surface. Turn the plant out into the palm of your hand with the stem between your fingers to catch and retain as much dirt as possible. If the root systems of any seedlings have filled the container, be sure to loosen any encircling roots at the bottom and side surfaces by pulling them gently away from the dirt mass and spreading them out in a hole large enough not to cramp them. If setting out a seedling in a peat pot, remove the top inch of the pot and set the soil in the pot even with the soil in the bed. Set the seedling at recommended intervals at the same soil depth at which it had been growing; backfill, gently firm in, and water well. Water in vegetable seedlings with a weak solution of water-soluble fertilizer. Pinch back the top growth of annual and perennial seedlings to encourage root growth and bushiness. Try to plant on an overcast day and shade seedlings from direct sun (or late frosts) for several days with baskets, planting trays, or newspapers.

Sowing outdoors. In well-prepared soil, make a furrow with the back of a rake or the tip of a trowel. Plant seeds at the depth recommended on the seed package. Or, in cool weather, plant seeds to a depth approximately three times the thickness of the seed lying down in the soil. Increase this to four times in warm weather. Mix fine seeds with sand for even distribution. Cover the seeds with fine soil to the suggested depth and tamp down lightly with a rake or the palm of your hand. Keep seed beds moist at all times with a fine mist so as not to dislodge the seeds until germination is complete.

GRASS

Seeding a new lawn. Rake and cultivate to 6 inches; enrich the soil with peat moss, compost, or leaf mold. Level the area to be planted. Apply lawn fertilizer lightly over the entire area. With a spreader, first sow half the seeds over the entire area, then sow the other half over the same area at right angles for complete coverage. Mulch with straw and roll. Sprinkle daily until the seeds sprout, then water thoroughly once or twice a week. Spring and fall are the best times to start a lawn from seed.

Sodding a new lawn. As an alternative to seeding, lay sod in strips on a freshly raked, clean dirt surface. Make sure the edges are touching. Roll and water thoroughly upon installation and thereafter once or twice a week. Avoid walking on a newly sodded lawn for three weeks. Sod can be laid throughout the growing season.

Replanting an established lawn. Rake the lawn thoroughly to remove thatch (dead grass), winter debris, and weeds. Level bumps and dips, rake the surface, and reseed bare spots. Keep planted areas moist by regular sprinkling until the grass has sprouted. Spring and fall are the best times to renew a lawn.

VEGETABLES AND HERBS

Plant perennial vegetables and herbs (asparagus, rhubarb, horseradish, rosemary, fennel) as you would plant any perennial. Plant annual vegetables and herbs as you would plant seeds or seedlings.

How to maximize space and production

- Prepare the garden in the fall for early spring planting of peas; cover that portion of the bed with black plastic. Tack it down with stones or logs. In early spring, remove the plastic, give the soil a light raking, and plant.
- Start vegetables and herbs indoors in early spring or in a nursery bed in summer to quickly fill empty spots.
- Plant fast-maturing vegetables (lettuce, mustard greens, radishes, spinach) between slow-maturing ones (eggplant, peppers, tomatoes). Try radishes in rows of carrots or parsley, early lettuce between broccoli seedlings or tomato plants.

☙ Lengthen the harvest period by sowing short rows of the same vegetable at weekly intervals but in different areas. Follow leafy, or top, crops with a root crop.

☙ As you harvest one crop, plant another. For example, beets, carrots, or broccoli follow peas. Peppers follow spring lettuce. Fall spinach follows carrots. Bush beans follow spinach, and a fall crop of carrots or beets completes the succession.

☙ Create extra space by planting in containers: vegetables with modest root systems will be the most successful (carrots, eggplant, lettuce, onions, peppers, dwarf varieties of tomato). Try dwarf hybrid cucumbers and tomatoes. Herbs flourish in containers. Rampant ones like mint can be kept under control. Many are tolerant of dry conditions. They are also attractive in plantings of mixed varieties and interspersed with annuals in the flower garden.

This huge clay pot holds several strawberry plants.

PRUNING

Most plants, if properly chosen and planted, will not need heavy pruning. Pruning, a means of plant discipline, is done to control the size and shape of plants, to stimulate new growth, or to remove dead, diseased, crossing, or damaged wood. Major pruning is best performed in the winter when plants are dormant and the temperature is above freezing. Pruning involves two techniques: heading back and thinning out. Many pruning situations require the use of both methods. Other techniques for controlling plant growth are limbing up, pinching back, and deadheading.

Heading back creates a dense, formal look. Remove the end of a branch to cause multiple branching out below the cut. Always cut just above a bud to avoid long stubs. New growth will follow the direction of the bud, so choose a bud pointing outward to discourage crossing branches. Use for hedges and topiary.

Thinning out enhances and maintains the natural shape of the plant. Remove a whole branch back to a main branch or trunk. This opens up the plant to air and light. Growth will continue from the terminal bud at the end of the main branch. Use for shade trees, fruit trees, and bushes.

Limbing up, or removing lower branches, root suckers, or water sprouts on trees and shrubs, allows more light into heavily shaded areas, increases air circulation, and reveals the trunk and branching structure of plants and interesting, colorful, or exfoliating bark. Use for small trees or large shrubs.

Pinching back delays flowering, promotes plant vigor, and results in thicker plants. Remove the growing point (terminal flower or leaf bud) by pinching it out by hand at regular intervals during the growing season. Use to control shrubs, annuals, perennials, and herbs.

Deadheading means removing spent flowers regularly to prevent seedpods from forming. With annuals it promotes continuous bloom, and with perennials rebloom. When deadheading bulbs, remove spent blossoms to prevent seed formation, which saps the strength of the bulbs for the following year. Leave foliage for a minimum of six weeks to wither and turn yellow before removing it.

☙ When and why to prune

DECIDUOUS, BROADLEAF EVERGREEN SHRUBS AND TREES

Spring-blooming. These plants bloom on wood that formed last year. Prune after they bloom to encourage next year's bloom and enhance the natural shape. Some spring-bloomers are azaleas, forsythia, hydrangea, mock orange, quince, rhododendron, spirea, and winter jasmine.

Summer-blooming. These plants bloom on wood produced during the same growing season. Prune in late winter to encourage bloom and enhance the natural shape. Some summer-bloomers are abelia, althaea, butterfly bush, crape myrtle, hypericum, shrub roses, and vitex.

Overgrown plants. Prune just before the spring growth spurt. Thin out old wood over a three-year period. Cut one-third of old, thick stems at the base each year and remove all dead and twiggy branchlets. This will rejuvenate a plant. Or cut deciduous shrubs to the ground and let them start again. If the tree or shrub is a spring-bloomer, the flowers will be sacrificed, but only for the next season. New growth will be rapid because the mature root system will put all of its energy into the production of new wood.

Roses. Prune most established shrub roses in early spring as soon as buds begin to swell. After removing all dead, weak, diseased, and crossing wood, cut all remaining canes back by one-third. Prune to maintain the desired height and shape of the plant and to keep the center of the shrub open for good air circulation. Make all cuts on a slant 1/4 inch above a strong and preferably outside bud. Prune old-fashioned rambler roses and rampant climbing roses after they bloom. Remove two-thirds of recently flowered wood to make way for new canes, which will produce blooms next year. Cut laterals back to eight to ten buds.

Hedges. Prune deciduous hedges in late winter by shearing with clippers to create a dense, formal look.

NEEDLE EVERGREEN SHRUBS AND TREES
Prune to maintain size and balance, preferably just before a growth spurt, so that new cuts will be covered quickly. Pine and spruce have one growth period, which is in spring. Arborvitae, hemlock, and juniper have a second spurt in midsummer and may require a second trimming. Do not prune in early fall because new growth stimulated by pruning will not have time to harden off before winter.

Hedges. Prune evergreen hedges by hand in early spring, just before a growth spurt, so that new cuts will be quickly covered. Trim hedges so that the top is narrower than the bottom to admit light to the base of the plants.

TOPIARY
Topiary is the shaping and training of twiggy plants, such as boxwood, Japanese hollies, privet, or yew, into fanciful animal or architectural shapes (dome, pyramid, or pillar) by constant clipping and pruning. Because topiary needs full sun, keep the top narrower than the bottom to admit light to the bottom of the plant.

ESPALIER
Espalier or train a small tree or shrub to grow flat against a wall, fence, or trellis by removing the rear and front branches of the plant. Spread and fasten the remaining branches against a wall. Nip out

terminal buds when the espalier reaches the proper width and height. Keep tightly trimmed. Prune just before the spring growth spurt and again in midsummer.

FRUIT TREES, GRAPEVINES, AND BERRY BUSHES
Many of these plants produce fruit only on new wood. Prune in mid- to late winter when dormant to encourage new growth and fruit production, and to balance and distribute the fruit load. Ask your local gardening center for special pruning requirements of specific varieties.

FERTILIZING

❦ *Understanding the fertilizer label*

Fertilizer comes from two sources: organic (natural) and synthetic (chemical). Organic fertilizers, including compost, leaf mold, aged manure, bonemeal, and blood meal, are used to enrich the soil, improve its texture, and provide good sources of trace elements as well as the basic elements of nitrogen, phosphorus, and potassium. They supply a slow, steady diet but have the disadvantage of being bulky and therefore hard to work with and store. Aged manure can be "brewed" to make manure tea, which is useful for watering in seedlings and small plants and is easier to apply than other, bulky organic fertilizers. Add several inches of aged or dehydrated manure to a pail of water. Allow the mixture to sit for several hours and apply as a liquid fertilizer.

Synthetic fertilizers are easier to find, store, and use. They come in many formulas and forms: liquid, powder, and granules. Unless the fertilizer is manufactured to be slow-release, the nutrients are readily available and are designed for rapid absorption directly into the plant. Water-soluble fertilizers provide nutrients most quickly. A disadvantage of synthetic fertilizers is that they wash out of the soil, especially in containers, and need to be applied more frequently. Also, they add no organic matter to improve soil texture and can burn plants if overused and allowed to build up in the soil.

The numbers on the label give the percentages of nitrogen, phosphorus, and potassium contained in the fertilizer. Therefore, 5-10-5 means 20 percent active ingredients and 80 percent filler, with the following active ingredients:

5%	nitrogen (N): a leaf stimulant that promotes rapid growth and green color.
10%	phosphorus (P): a bloom and seed stimulant that promotes fruit production.
5%	potassium (K): a root stimulant that promotes general well-being and winter-hardiness
————	
20%	

A complete fertilizer would be 5-10-5 or 10-10-10. An incomplete fertilizer would be 0-10-0 or 0-20-10. If you need a high-nitrogen fertilizer, look for one that has the first number higher than the other two; for a high-phosphorus fertilizer, look for one with the middle number the highest; for a high-potassium fertilizer, look for one with the third number the highest.

A well-clipped garden.

❦ Soil pH

The pH scale, which ranges from 0 to 14, is a way of measuring the acidity or alkalinity of soil. Zero indicates the maximum acidity and 14 the maximum alkalinity. A reading of 7 is neutral. A soil test will determine the pH of your soil and how to correct it if necessary. Proper pH balance is essential to enable plants to absorb the nutrients from the soil that ensure proper growth. Most plants prefer a neutral to slightly acid soil. The major exceptions are ericaceous and other acid-loving plants (azaleas, blueberries, camellias, heather, hollies, hydrangeas, leucothoe, deciduous magnolias, mountain laurel, pieris, and rhododendrons), which prefer a pH of 4.5–5.5

ADJUSTING SOIL pH

- ❦ *To raise pH:* add lime (ground or dolomitic limestone).
- ❦ *To lower pH:* add sulfur, iron sulfate, aluminum sulfate, acid-reacting fertilizer, sawdust, or acid peat moss.

SOIL TESTING

For information, call your county agricultural agent or Cooperative Extension agent, listed under "U.S. Government, Department of Agriculture," in the telephone book. Some state universities and many garden centers provide this service. You can buy a do-it-yourself kit with instructions, but home-use kits are not as reliable as agricultural agents.

❦ When and how to fertilize

Most nursery and container-grown stock does not require fertilizer at planting time. To determine what fertilizer is needed to maintain established plants or when transplanting within the garden, consult the following section. Choose the right fertilizer for the job. Read labels carefully and apply fertilizers according to directions. Keep fertilizers away from the stems and leaves of plants and the trunks of trees. Never fertilize dry soils, and water thoroughly after applying to settle granules and start nutrients toward the feeder roots.

TREES

Mature. Use high-nitrogen tree spikes or have an arborist deep-root feed the trees if they show signs of stress or poor leaf color.

Immature. Use high-nitrogen granular fertilizer (12-6-6) in early spring; broadcast evenly beneath the drip line of the tree.

Fruit. Use high-nitrogen granular fertilizer (12-6-6) in early spring; broadcast evenly beneath the drip line of the tree. Feed again after flowering.

SHRUBS

Use high-phosphorus granular fertilizer (5-10-5) in early spring; broadcast evenly beneath the canopy of the plant. Feed again after flowering. Use the high-acid version of 5-10-5 on acid-loving plants.

Roses. Roses are heavy feeders. Feed monthly with rose fertilizer until six weeks before the first expected frost.

GRASS

Cool-season grasses. Apply a high-nitrogen fertilizer (24-4-8) in early spring and again in late spring; repeat in late summer and again in the fall after the ground freezes to promote root growth.

Warm-season grasses. Apply a balanced fertilizer (10-10-10) in early spring and again in late fall, or monthly on heavily irrigated lawns.

Apply lime in the fall if pH is below 6.0 or 7.0.

When applying "weed-and-feed" products, use caution. Be sure to choose the correct product for your grass type and apply at the specified time.

GROUND COVERS

Sprinkle ground-cover beds (ivy, pachysandra, vinca, winter creeper) with granular 5-10-5 or work in dehydrated manure in early spring.

PERENNIALS
Use high-phosphorus granular fertilizer (5-10-5) or aged or dehydrated manure in early spring in a ring around each plant as it emerges.

ANNUALS
Incorporate a continuous-release fertilizer into the soil at planting time and fertilize every three to four weeks during the growing season with a water-soluble, balanced fertilizer (10-10-10).

BULBS
Feed bulbs at planting time with bulb food or 10-10-10 fertilizer, and again in the early spring as foliage begins to emerge. Summer- and fall-blooming bulbs should be fed at half the recommended rates each month until their foliage begins to fade. Fertilize belladonna lilies, colchicum, and lycoris when in leaf, not when in bloom.

VEGETABLES
Use water-soluble foliar fertilizer or manure tea at transplanting time or when leafy vegetables show signs of yellowing leaves. To fertilize established vegetables, side-dress, or spread, an even row of fertilizer down each side of a row, or encircle the plant. Work carefully into the soil and water thoroughly.

HERBS
Most herbs, if planted in moderately rich, well-drained soil, do not need summer fertilizing. Instead, dig a small amount of compost into established beds each fall.

GRAPEVINES, BERRY BUSHES, AND STRAWBERRIES
Use balanced granular fertilizer (10-10-10) in a ring around each established plant in early spring or when planting. Feed again after harvesting.

GARDENING TOOLS AND SUPPLIES

Buy good-quality tools and keep them clean, dry, sharpened, and oiled as necessary. Occasionally apply a thin coat of oil to wooden handles to keep them smooth. When storing tools for the winter, lightly oil metal surfaces as well as wooden handles.

Buy only enough fungicides and insecticides for one season. If necessary, store any remaining liquids in a frost-free location. Keep all these materials out of reach of children, clearly labeled, and preferably in a locked closet. Any spraying equipment should be thoroughly washed after each use. Empty the gasoline tank and drain the fuel lines of mechanical equipment before storing.

❦ The basics for a small garden

spade
shovel
fork—square-tined for heavy soil
rakes
    metal for cultivating
    bamboo or plastic for leaf raking
garden trowel, transplanting trowel
hand fork
hand cultivator
pruning clippers, shears, loppers, saw
asparagus knife (good for weeding)
lawn mower
water equipment
    hoses: nylon-reinforced garden hoses and soaker hoses
    sprinklers
    adjustable nozzle, mister, bubbler
    watering can
    rain gauge
plant labels, stakes, twine, indelible-ink pen
espalier nails and coated wire
gardening gloves
fungicides and insecticides
plant and garden sprayers
    gloves, goggles, disposable overalls
    respirator if applying toxic chemicals
fertilizers and soil amendments
    aged or dehydrated manure
    peat moss
compost bin
mulch
soil-test kit

❦ Extras for a large garden

wheelbarrow or garden cart
irrigation system
    drip-irrigation system that uses emitters
    mini-sprinklers that apply water to plant root zones
    automatic system that uses timers
sprayer for insecticides and fungicides
    portable sprayer with built-in pump action, or
    compressed-air sprayer
    separate sprayer for weed control
pole pruner
cold frame
shredder/grinder for garden waste

🍎 Just for the vegetable garden

power tiller for large gardens
hoe
cultivator
tomato cages
stakes, poles, trellises
trellis netting
soil thermometer
mulch
    organic
    black plastic

🍎 Just for indoor gardening

smaller clippers, cultivating tools
watering can with rose nozzle
mister
grow lights
house-plant insecticides and fungicides, fertilizer
seed-starting supplies
    plastic or jiffy pots
    flats
    sterile potting soil
    bottom-heat coil

OUTDOOR-INDOOR GARDEN CARE

🍎 Adjuncts to good gardening

HOW TO BUILD A COMPOST PILE

Save all healthy garden refuse, dried leaves, salt hay and straw, lawn clippings, vegetable and fruit wastes, coffee grounds, and eggshells to build a compost pile. Keep the layers thin. Add a decomposition aid (available at garden centers), lawn fertilizer, or periodic layers of garden soil, and sprinkle with water to dampen. A minimum of 3 cubic feet is required to hold enough heat (160°) in the decomposing process to pasteurize the compost and kill most weed seeds, insects, and fungal diseases. Use the compost as a mulch or mix it with garden soil as an organic fertilizer and soil conditioner.

HOW TO INSTALL A COLD FRAME

Build or install a cold frame to get a head start on spring. A cold frame is a protective structure without a bottom that sits on the ground. It has a glass or plastic top that will open and shut. Sides may be made of wood, masonry, straw, bundled newspapers, or plastic sheeting stapled onto a wooden frame. The top is usually slanted

to catch the sun and drain rainwater away from the structure. Place in a southern exposure, protected from snowdrifts and wind. Use for starting annuals, perennials, and vegetables from seed for the spring or summer garden; for hardening off seedlings; for sowing late-fall or winter crops; and for overwintering hardy vegetables, tender perennials, and potted herbs.

❧ Basic maintenance

HOW TO WATER

Lack of water causes stress in plants and endangers their health. Water in the early morning or late afternoon to reduce evaporation during the heat of the day. If you water late in the day, avoid spraying water directly on the foliage, which encourages fungi, mold, and mildew to develop on wet leaves during the night. During a severe water shortage, establish priorities: water trees, shrubs, and lawns, respectively. Pay attention to newly installed plants, which are at highest risk. Plants have different moisture requirements at different stages of development.

Seeds need constant moisture to germinate. Sprinkle the soil surface once or twice a day.

Seedlings and transplants, which have shallow root development, need frequent, light waterings.

Deep-rooted plants, shrubs, and trees grow best with deep but less frequent watering.

Newly planted stock is especially vulnerable until thoroughly established (as long as two to three years for major trees and shrubs). Supplement inadequate rainfall with additional waterings by hand, or use soaker hoses or drip irrigation to conserve water. Keep drops off foliage to prevent fungus. Clay soil, which retains water and impedes its passage, requires deep, slow watering, but avoid overwatering in areas with "caliche" soil or hardpan. Sandy soil, which drains quickly, requires more frequent waterings. Wind and high temperatures dry out plant material and soil more rapidly. Water if the soil is dry below the surface or if plants are withered in the morning or evening. Do not water in the heat of the day. Water thoroughly (light sprinkling results in development of shallow roots). Water year-round in areas lacking snow coverage or adequate winter rains. To conserve water, form earthen saucers around larger plants when planting. Use stones or natural-looking stakes as bed edgers to prevent the hose from dragging through the beds and crushing plants.

Lawns. Sprinkle newly seeded lawns daily until seeds sprout, then twice a week until the lawn is established at mowing height. Once a lawn is established, water by soaking weekly to encourage deep roots, then water again only when the surface soil is dry.

HOW TO MULCH

Mulching helps to keep soil temperatures constant and to keep moisture in the ground and weeds out. Some mulches amend the soil's chemistry (pine needles and oak leaves acidify soil); others increase its friability and fertility (decomposing mulches add humus and organic matter). Some mulches, such as pebbles or crushed stone, not only conserve moisture, make a neater-looking planting, and aid drainage, but are long lasting.

Mulch in summer to reduce watering and soil crusting, to discourage weeds, and to lower soil temperatures in the root zone. Choose a texture that complements the plant. Apply 2–3 inches deep. Try cocoa and buckwheat hulls, cottonseed meal, shredded leaves, leafy compost, pine needles, shredded bark, bark nuggets, sugarcane pulp, salt hay, or straw. Use grass clippings if the grass has not been sprayed with herbicides and if clippings have aged several weeks.

Mulch in winter to prevent thawing and freezing of the ground and subsequent heaving of small and newly installed plants, and to prevent moisture loss and freeze damage to roots of tender plants. Apply 4–8 inches deep after the ground freezes. Try shredded leaves, leafy compost, pine needles, shredded bark, bark nuggets, salt hay, straw, or boughs from discarded Christmas trees. Lay down small branches to keep the mulch in place in windy spots. Remove winter mulches as the soil warms up in the spring.

HOW TO STAKE

Try "pea staking" for a more natural look, using twiggy branches pruned from trees and shrubs as stakes. Place them in the ground among the plants as they begin to grow. Their combined mass creates stability. Or use commercial stakes, which come in many sizes. When tying a tall perennial or vegetable to a stake, be sure the stake

is strong. Fasten soft twine or old cloth securely to the stake first, then tie the plant loosely to avoid damaging the stem.

HOW TO WEED

Avoid disturbing shallow-rooted plants (most annuals, perennials, and vegetables) while weeding. Weed after a rain or thorough watering, especially when pulling weeds. Snip out unwanted seedlings with scissors to avoid disturbing adjacent plants or latent weed seeds. Remove weeds with a taproot—a long, central, vertical root—by cutting under the soil surface with an old kitchen knife or asparagus knife. Weed before the weeds set seed and multiply. Most woody plants will tolerate rougher treatment, including light cultivation with a hose in the planting bed. Thoroughly weed all beds in the fall.

HOW TO CUT FLOWERS FOR DRYING

Gather flowers before they are in full bloom, in the early morning after the dew has dried. For variety, gather blooms at different stages of maturity. Collect only undamaged specimens of different sizes, shapes, colors, and textures. Strip off lower leaves; bind smaller flowers in bunches with a rubber band because stems will shrink; hang upside down in a warm, dry, well-ventilated spot. Larger flowers should hang separately. Plumes like astilbe, goldenrod, and heather may be dried upright in bottles or vases. Delicate grasses maintain their shape better if dried flat. Flowers are dry when their stems, particularly near the blossom, feel dry and crisp. This may take 3–5 weeks. To protect colors, store in a dark spot until ready to use.

FALL CLEANUP

- Lawn care: continue mowing and watering new grass; lawn should be 2 inches high as winter begins; rake lawn regularly or the leaves will mat and smother the grass.
- Compost leaves; add a layer of lime or lawn fertilizer to hasten decomposition.
- Dispose of foliage of dogwood, gladiolus, iris, and peonies, and any other leaves showing signs of disease.
- Prepare flower and vegetable gardens for spring planting: dig deeply, enrich with compost and strawy manure, spread lime if a soil test indicates a too acidic soil. Cover early-spring planting areas with black plastic or salt hay.
- Clean up perennial beds.
- Remove annuals and compost.
- Weed, shape, and edge beds.
- Clean up and dispose of all fallen rose leaves under bushes. Mound 10–12 inches of extra dirt around roses to protect from winter damage.
- Prune and fasten climbers against wind damage.
- Lift tuberous begonias, caladiums, cannas, dahlias, gladiolus, tritoma, and other tender bulbs after first frost; dust with sulfur and store in vermiculite in a cool cellar.

❦ Bring house plants indoors.

❦ Empty and store terra-cotta containers.

❦ Protect warm-season vegetables if frost is predicted.

❦ Update records of planting and harvesting dates. List gaps in planting, favorite varieties, quantity and quality of harvest. Make a crop-rotation plan for next year.

❦ In cold regions, ventilate cold frames until ground has frozen; close and mulch lightly or cover with straw matting.

❦ Water shallow-rooted plants, such as dogwoods, broadleaf evergreens, newly planted trees, and newly planted bulb beds, thoroughly before ground freezes.

❦ Clean and prepare bird feeders.

❦ Feed fish in lily ponds until water freezes.

❦ Clean gutters and downspouts.

❦ Turn off water, drain hoses, service irrigation systems, store garden furniture.

WINTER PLANT PROTECTION

❦ Water newly planted and established broadleaf and needle evergreens during the January thaw or winter dry season.

❦ Spray broadleaf evergreens with antidesiccant to prevent foliage dehydration when temperature is above 40°; repeat during midwinter.

❦ After the ground freezes, mulch bulb beds, perennials, and other small plants to prevent heaving during periods of thawing and freezing.

❦ Interweave and encircle boxwood and other brittle shrubs with twine, or install covers and tie ropes around columnar plants to prevent snow damage.

❦ Check guy wires on newly planted trees; tighten if heaved by frost.

❦ Check trees and shrubs for rodent damage; protect with wire mesh or tree wrap.

❦ Set snow fences.

❦ Use sand or ashes on icy walks and drives—salt damages plantings and lawns.

❦ To prevent bare spots on next spring's lawn, avoid walking on frozen grass.

❦ Shake and sweep snow from evergreens; let ice covering melt naturally.

❦ Move half-hardy container plants into the greenhouse or cold frame, or, in warmer regions, sink in the ground for winter protection.

❦ Cover marginally hardy plants with burlap, leaves, or baskets if a freeze is predicted. Remove the coverings as temperatures rise.

❦ Propagation techniques

HOW TO DIVIDE

Perennials. Cut a circle around the plant with a digging fork. Get under and lift the entire mass. Cut or gently pull apart the crowded clumps. Discard the woody central portion and any diseased or stunted parts. Cut the tops back to 6 inches. Replant the healthy divisions in areas well prepared with peat moss, compost, or leaf mold. Water well to settle. In general, divide spring- and summer-blooming perennials in late summer or fall; fall- and winter-blooming perennials in spring. Many can be divided in either spring or fall.

Ground covers. Cut a 6-inch piece of the plant that includes a portion of its root system. Dip it in a rooting hormone and plant it to fill in bare spots in existing beds or to start new beds. Prepare the soil well in advance, mulch, and set ground-cover divisions through the mulch at 8-inch intervals and at the same depth at which they were previously growing.

Shrubs. Divide multistemmed shrubs by pushing a sharp spade down to both sever and lift a portion of the plant, or dig the entire plant, cut or saw through the root system, and replant each individual healthy section.

HOW TO TAKE SOFTWOOD CUTTINGS

During the growing season, take 2–4 inches from the terminal growth of trees, shrubs, or perennials. The shoots should be mature enough to snap when bent double. Cut slightly on a diagonal below a leaf node, where the leaf joins the stem. Place cuttings in a plastic bag or bucket of water immediately to prevent them from drying out, and store in a shaded spot. When planting, remove all but two or three leaves, dip the butt end in rooting hormone, and insert it in a rooting medium of equal parts sphagnum, peat moss, and builder's sand or vermiculite in a flat. Keep moist at all times, misting regularly until cuttings are well rooted. Cuttings can be covered with clear plastic to conserve moisture. Set in bright light, but avoid direct sun. Once the cuttings have rooted in four to six weeks, transplant them to individual pots. Gradually move them into brighter light until they can tolerate full sun. When new growth begins, set transplants into the garden or a nursery bed.

HOW TO TAKE HARDWOOD CUTTINGS

After leaf fall, when plants are almost dormant, take cuttings 6–10 inches long, three to four buds per section, from wood of the current year's growth. Cut slightly on a diagonal just below a bud at the bottom of each cutting. Bury vertically, butt end down, in slightly moist sand, peat moss, or sawdust, and store in a cool cellar (40°–45°). A callus will form over the butt end. In early spring when the ground is workable, remove cuttings from storage and plant out in nursery rows. Set cuttings so that only the tip shows above the soil. By fall, cuttings should be well rooted and ready to transplant to permanent quarters.

HOW TO LAYER

During spring and early summer, layer woody-stemmed shrubs such as cotoneaster, forsythia, junipers, magnolia, some rhododendrons, periwinkle *(Vinca minor),* and other ground covers. These plants have a tendency to root readily when their branches come in contact with the soil. Bend a one-year-old, flexible branch to the ground and cover with a layer of soil, first removing any foliage that might be buried. Woody branches should be scraped or notched at the point where the branch and dirt meet. Dust with rooting hormone. Cover the contact area with a layer of soil and keep it in place with a forked stick or small stone. In spring, when the new plant is established, sever it from the parent plant and transplant it the following spring.

❦ House-plant care

WINTER

Enjoy indoor gardening during winter months. Select house plants with care. Try to replicate their native habitats, which indicate their cultural requirements. Most foliage plants are native to tropical jungles and rain forests. They prefer diffused natural light and will not tolerate direct sun, especially at midday. All house plants need:

Adequate light. Augment with fluorescent or grow lights if necessary. Turn plants frequently in the window for even light.

Correct daytime and nighttime temperatures. The average range should be 62°–75°. Avoid drafts and sudden chills. Pull pots back from icy windows at night or place newspapers against the glass.

Water. Pour tepid water until it runs out the bottom of the pot. Drain excess water from the saucer, or set the pot in a basin to absorb water until the soil surface is damp, and then drain excess water. If in doubt about watering, press your finger into the soil—moist soil will cling to your skin. If still in doubt, wait a day. Waterlogged soil prevents entry of essential oxygen to the root system. Do not overwater; it causes root rot.

Humidity. Increase humidity around plants. Set them in a tray of moist pebbles above, not in, the water. Group pots together and mulch with sphagnum moss. Mist daily.

Fertilizer. Feed plants monthly with fish emulsion or water-soluble house-plant fertilizer—full strength during spring and summer when in active growth, half-strength during fall and winter when dormant. Read the label. Do not apply fertilizer to dry soil.

Grooming. Each week, remove dead and diseased foliage; pinch back to shape as necessary. Shower plants in the sink or gently sponge leaves to keep them clean. Keep pots, saucers, and pebbles clean.

Treatment for insect or disease problems. Use household insecticidal soap or house-plant insect sprays and fungicides. Dunk small plants in a bucket of diluted soapy water. Remove scale with a cotton swab dipped in alcohol.

Repotting and dividing. Repot when plant roots fill the available soil in the pot, roots emerge through drainage holes, watering becomes increasingly necessary, or when the plant looks out of scale and top-heavy in its pot. Dampen the root ball and remove it from the container. Repot it in a container several inches larger in diameter if you want the plant to continue to grow, or scrub the existing pot free of salts and plant in the same container if you want to keep the plant the same size. In both cases, cut around the fibrous root ball, trim roots, tease some roots apart, or unwind and prune thick roots to stimulate healthy growth. If dividing, cut with a clean, sharp knife into two or more portions, maintaining one or more stems with each division. Repot in commercially bagged soil that has been sterilized and will not introduce insects and diseases. Water well and shade from direct sun until reestablished.

SPRING THROUGH SUMMER

In late spring, as nighttime temperatures stabilize at around 68°, start moving cool-temperature house plants outside to a protected, semishady spot. Wait for the temperature to reach 75° before moving tropical plants. Sink pots into the ground or group together to conserve moisture. Water as necessary. Check frequently for insects and diseases. Turn pots sunk in the ground to sever escaping roots, and turn all pots for even development.

FALL

As evenings become chilly, bring tropical plants indoors. Cool-temperature, flowering plants can remain outdoors for several more weeks. They require a light frost and shortened days to set buds. All require time to become accustomed to the lower light and humidity levels indoors before the heat goes on.

Divide overgrown plants. Cut back on watering and feeding as plants go into dormancy. Turn frequently for even development.

Check all plants for insects and diseases. Spray each plant once a week for three consecutive weeks with insecticidal soap before bringing it indoors. Do this in the shade to avoid burning the plants. Take cuttings, trim, and repot. Scrub pots and saucers. If potting soil is harboring insects, soak the pot, roots and all, in a bucket of water mixed with a tablespoon of Sevin, a broad-spectrum insecticide containing cabaryl. Spray and encase plants in a plastic bag for fumigation. Keep plastic off the foliage and set the plants out of the sun.

CONTROLLING INSECTS AND DISEASES

An innovative approach to a healthy garden is Integrated Pest Management, or IPM. IPM stresses sound cultural practices and the switch from toxic chemicals to natural and biological controls because pests are becoming increasingly immune and chemicals are disastrous to the environment.

A garden with a diverse population of plants is more resistant to insects and disease than a monoculture—a crop of single species—because it is less likely to suffer a large infestation of a particular

pest. As plants are more susceptible to insect and disease when under stress, make every effort to maintain the health of your plants. Keep a neat and clean garden to reduce insect hiding places. Plant disease- and insect-resistant plants, especially in the vegetable garden, and observe the proper spacing, siting, and installation of plants. The correct maintenance of your plants—fertilizing, watering, and mulching—as well as the timing of pruning and the thorough cleanup of fallen leaves, plays a role in the prevention and control of pest problems.

Monitor your garden year-round. By checking regularly for the appearance of insects and diseases, by identifying key pests and observing pest-prone plants, you can handle the majority of pest problems without resorting to environmentally unfriendly or hazardous treatments. Identify problems correctly and treat them promptly before they become too great. Remove and burn or bag diseased plant material.

🍒 Identify the problem

1. **Identify the plant.** Insects and diseases are specific to many plants at certain times of the year. Knowing the name of the plant and its common afflictions will help you identify the pest.

2. **Identify the insect.** Many insects are clearly visible on the undersides of leaves, tunneling in leaves, or in cocoons or webs. Keep garden records of the approximate arrival and departure dates of insects. Weather may affect the timing of their appearance each year, but insects are predictable in their habits.

3. **Identify a bacterial or fungal disease.** Look for such symptoms as stem and root rot, wilt, putrid fruits, random dead or off-color spots in leaves, off-color and curled leaf edges, powdery mildew or scale, and sudden dieback of branches. Symptoms are often more intense during wet springs, in overwatered soil, or in areas with poor air circulation.

4. **Identify environmental stress.**

DROUGHT: wilting on new growth in late afternoon, loss or yellowing of foliage, dieback or leaf scorch on current season's leaves. Water deeply and thoroughly (1 inch per week). Amend soil to encourage water retention; mulch well. In drought conditions, thin heavily foliated plants to cut back on transpiration.

POOR DRAINAGE: caused by poor irrigation systems, compacted soil, construction damage, or a grade change that has buried important feeder roots. Discolored, wilted leaves and mildew are symptoms of either poor drainage or overwatering. In new beds, amend soil with sand or gravel. In established beds, correct destructive drainage patterns.

SUNSCALD: burning and cracking of tender, smooth bark on newly planted trees. Provide light shade or wrap the trunk to protect it. Avoid reflected heat and light from buildings or paving. Choose heat-tolerant plants.

WINTER BURN OR FREEZE DAMAGE: caused by sudden drops in temperature. Results in bud, leaf, and fruit drop; dieback of tender new growth; and on evergreens, brown tips on previous season's growth apparent in spring. Move tender plants to shelter or provide temporary protection.

IRON DEFICIENCY (chlorosis): leaves turn yellow, starting between veins of the young growth while veins remain green. May be caused by high pH. Test soil, correct pH, spray with water-soluble iron or dig iron chelates into soil.

CHEMICAL DAMAGE: leaf discoloration, poor growth, dieback. May be caused by swimming pool chemicals. Store and mix chemicals away from planted areas. Prevent pool backwash from reaching plantings. Use spray weed killers with caution to keep drift from falling on desirable plants.

SALT BUILDUP: poor growth, loss of leaf luster. Caused by runoff from highways or sidewalks, ocean winds. Rinse salt-sprayed plants with water in early morning and irrigate heavily to leach out accumulation of salts. Choose salt-tolerant varieties in beach areas and along roadways where salt is spread to melt winter ice.

🍒 Choose the solution

Timing is crucial in the application of pesticides. Learn everything you can about the life cycle of insects as they are more vulnerable at certain developmental stages, such as larval or nymph, than at others. Weather may affect the timing of their appearance. Use pesticides as a last resort. Read the labels carefully and spray conservatively. Mix only what you need to use for the day. Do not use sprays when the temperature is over 80° or under 40°. Spray in calm weather, either early in the morning or late in the day. Keep in mind that any spray potent enough to kill undesirable insects is likely to kill something else. Rotate your use of chemicals wherever practical. Beware of pesticides that can harm birds, animals, and beneficial insects. Take great care in using any toxic materials in the vegetable garden. Systemic sprays and slug pellets are not suitable for use on edible plants. To avoid killing pollinating bees, do not spray citrus or other fruit while in bloom. Do not use pesticides (insecticides, miticides, or fungicides) in a sprayer previously used for weed control.

Call your county agent or local Cooperative Extension Service for more information on controlling pest problems.

IN THE FLOWER GARDEN

- Use a strong blast of water from the hose to wash off aphids, mites, and other insects.
- Prune out planted areas heavily infested with egg nests.
- Encourage friendly bugs and natural predatory insects, such as pollinating bees, lacewings, aphid-eating ladybugs, and praying mantis, which have a varied insect diet.
- Plant strong-smelling herbs and flowers among other plants to help control garden insects.

IN THE VEGETABLE GARDEN

- Spread diatomaceous earth (used in swimming-pool filters), ashes, and pine-needle mulch to deter crawling insects.
- Use fine mesh and spun polyester fabric to protect fruits and vegetables from birds and egg-laying, flying insects.
- Use mechanical devices such as cutworm collars, tarpaper mats, aluminum-foil disks, and fly traps to deter and trap insects.
- Plant different species to discourage widespread infestations. Rotate disease- and insect-prone plants so that an area does not become heavily infested with soilborne diseases. Choose resistant plant varieties.
- Rest a difficult area over the winter by planting a cover crop, such as alfalfa, annual rye, clover, or vetch, and turning it under in spring to enrich the soil.
- Leave one or two favored plants, such as mustard, cabbage, or horseradish, as hosts or catch plants, which will attract insects away from more desirable plants. Plant radishes as a sacrifice crop among root crops to attract root maggots away from other roots. Handpick and destroy individual insects. Allow host plants and sacrifice crops to mature, then pull and destroy them.
- Make a general, all-purpose insect spray by blending water, garlic cloves, onion juice, and leaves of stinging nettles or hot peppers. Let stand twenty-four hours. Then dissolve 3/4 ounce of an oil-based soap in 1 pint of water, add to the vegetable mixture, and strain. It is ready for spraying.
- Use insecticidal soap and *Bacillus thuringiensis* to safely control pest problems without harming the environment and killing beneficial insects.
- Take great care in using any toxic materials in the vegetable garden. Systemic sprays and slug pellets are not suitable for use on edibles. To avoid killing pollinating bees, do not spray citrus or other fruit trees while in bloom. Do not use pesticides in a sprayer previously used for weed control.

INDOORS

- Spray or dunk afflicted house plants in a soap-and-water solution (do not use detergent), or wash with insecticidal soap; rinse with a spray of cool water. Repeat several times to get results. Or spray or wipe afflicted leaves with rubbing alcohol diluted with a little water.

Maintain a seasonal watch

WINTER (DORMANT SEASON)

Watch for signs of overwintering insects and diseases: insect eggs, scale, galls. Apply a dormant oil spray to smother dormant insects when the temperature is above 40°. In the vegetable garden, remove all debris and till the soil deeply to expose overwintering insects to cold temperatures. In warm climates, stir 5 percent Diazinon granules into the soil or use Diazinon as a soil soak before planting.

SPRING

Insects are beginning to appear. Identify and treat them promptly. Alert observation and treatment of insects and diseases at this stage of their development will simplify later care. As a preventive measure, begin a rose spray program as soon as new growth appears.

SUMMER

Insects and diseases are at their height. Spray, dust, and handpick regularly. Continuous maintenance and prevention are the best controls. Remove and dispose of debris from azaleas, camellias, and roses, which may harbor disease.

FALL

Insect problems lessen as plants harden off for the winter. Frosts kill many species. Clean up the garden thoroughly and dispose of any diseased plant material. Apply dormant oil spray in late fall or early winter.

AUTHORS

LOUISE CARTER, of Louise Carter - Garden Design, a residential garden design business in Wayne, Pennsylvania, is the author of *Basic Gardening,* published by Fulcrum Publishing in 1995. **JOANNE SEALE LAWSON** is a principal with Lawson Carter Epstein Landscape Architects in Washington, D.C., specializing in residential design. She is co-creator with Louise Carter of the *Gardener's Guide* calendar series published annually by Fulcrum Publishing.

PHOTOGRAPHER

ALLEN ROKACH is an internationally recognized garden photographer and a senior photographer at *Southern Living* magazine. His images and articles have appeared in *National Geographic, Audubon,* and *Natural History.* He lives in Birmingham, Alabama.